Number 1

EXQUISITE Corpse ANNUAL

www.corpse.org

A Journal of Letters and Life

EXQUISITE CORPSE ANNUAL NUMBER 1 2009

ISSN 1943-6122
ISBN-10 0615228577
ISBN-13 9780615228570

Printed in USA by Conway Printing Company Inc.,
Conway, AR.

A Journal of Letters and Life

INSIDE THE CORPSE

A Journal of Letters and Life

FROM THE EC CHAIR

by Andrei Codrescu

I founded *Exquisite Corpse: A Journal of Books & Letters* in Baltimore in 1983, in order to keep up with the work of writers I was interested in. I saw the *Corpse* in the lineage of avant-garde magazines, such as *transit*, and *The Little Review,* and closer to my own day, rebel poet-vehicles such as *Floating Bear*, edited by Diane Di Prima in New York and in San Francisco, and *The World*, published in the late Sixties and early Seventies by Anne Waldman and Lewish Warsh. Like the editors of those journals, I felt contempt for the boring pap flowing out of mainstream academic and publishing culture. In 1983, the vibrant poetry scenes of the past two decades were all but dead. The boring people were back in charge and the United States was being occupied by Ronald Reagan's zombies. Poetry, far from being seditious, was becoming a subject for writing programs. Critical discourse was at an all-time low, and the few of us who still had the energy to move, headed for the safe-houses of universities or journalism. In 1984 I took the *Exquisite Corpse* to LSU with me, but even though I was a professor of English there, the magazine was never an official university publication, and it never became one for the entire 25 years of my academic career. LSU did provide us with a graduate assistant who, generally, learned much from his or her editorial duties. Many of our assistants, among them Mark Spitzer, the managing editor of this Annual, went on to distinguished publishing, teaching, and writing careers. The mutual benefit that assured our independence survived quite a few ruffled conservative feathers over the years. There was also a staggering amount of work involved. We started in an age before computers, laying everything out in old-fashioned type, and pasting each issue by hand. The computers did help our layout some, but then we had a revelation: in 1996 we decided to become an internet publication, *corpse.org: a journal of life & letters.* There were not many internet journals at that time, blogging was still far in the future, and the academic world looked askance at internet-publishing. The internet has the last laugh now, but there are still many of our readers who miss the old print journal. Mark Spitzer suggested bringing out an *Exquisite Corpse Annual*, using material from the growing website at corpse.org, and soliciting work from writers we admire. Mark convinced UCA to back an annual anthology from our feisty little journal, without making editorial demands on our notorious independence. So here it is, folks, the *Exquisite Corpse Annual*, a retro print book that you can read in a cave with a headlamp. The *Annual* is not intended to replace *corpse.org,* which will go on. The *Annual* presents a choice selection of some of the *Corpse*'s best-known friends, on whom we called using only persuasion and charm, alas. We thank them from our hearts.

A CORPSE IS BORN

by Mark Spitzer

When Andrei and I discovered ourselves suddenly transplanted into the strange terrain of Arkansas, recollaboration was imminent. Via UCA, a new incarnation was conceived. Dean Rollin Potter, Dr. Scott Payne, and Warwick Sabin envisioned Exquisiteness—as did the UCA Foundation, who gave us a grant to kick things off. So now it's an honor to have jolly poet Terry Wright busting it out as Associate Ed., while the legendary Rex Rose scrambles as Design Guru. Meanwhile, Robin Becker represents, our Scanmaster is Tim Thornes, and Andrew Mobbs is helping me take it to the streets.

Viva La Corpse!

LOBA POETICS & MORE

by Diane di Prima

LOBA DESESPERADA

"When I sing as I please,
I taste blood in my mouth."
—Tia Anica la Piriñaca
Flamenco Singer

here at the dead end
of this final canyon
(have we at last
outwitted death)
this black hole
no water
only sheer rock opening
to a "V" of sky
where the sun
will find us
strike
& strike again
like a grim mother
Medea
of the stars

O Mother
was it for this I flew
headlong

lamp of Orion
like a miner's cap
at my brow
while I chipped
& chipped at stone walls
thru the night

& that lost caravan
of sleeping gypsies
my friends
turned to pointillist
dust
turned to so much
sand

no harpist
no silence melting to song
no final
flight
to the edge
of open space
only this cul-de-sac
blacker than any
night
blacker than jet
or onyx

where emptiness
of emptiness
shows her teeth
& at last
we love Her

in this black rock canyon
lost
waterhole
we wait for the sun
to suck the juice
from us

leave nails & hair
leave geometric bones
on shivering ground

2.

sifting darkness out of the night
like grains of black sand
from a midnight storm

SIEGE

(after Rilke)

1.
who
if I cry
breaks forth from
the Orders of Being?

Dominions
Thrones
Cherubim—
ranged as a wall
against
meaning. Against

the prayer of the heart

2.
Those who leave
shot as spies
Those
who stay
starving.

what order
under whose Orders?
the Seraphim?
Principalities.

These are the names
of Power
ranged
as a bastion against
Devotion.

3.
Only the single presence
single photon
streams home
to the heart of the
Master.

which of these ranged &
military
Selves

can break loose
can break
for Home?

still so far
there are
so many to be Named
before the Threshold.

4.
Each single Angel
terrible
as a photon
each stream
against & into

light

the Emptiness
of Light.

NOTE TO DUNCAN

1.
Ruthless.

It is ruthless.

And I am only happy
in its service.

2.
Surface.
The Work like a blind plant
breaks thru
the skin of the World.

MNEMOSYNE

All lost times / are one
& yet they differ
from one another
like the minds
of the Buddhas

clear crystal / taking its cast
from the time.
This almost white
amethyst, this
lucidity of
red,
blue,
emerald

laid aside they are all
the same when you take them

up
one differs from another
by a shadow
of a cast
of time

2.
by the shadow
of a shadow

of a cast
of time

that the most precious
that can be handed on

are syllables
often w/out meaning
& in precise order
"ear whispered"

cast
at a late age
from the realm of Song

like a small fish
stranded on the sand
while the sun
drinks
color
from her scales

DUENDE

He remembers them
as silver swords &
black lances

the women he loved.

Does not stop to ask
how they might
remember him.

MUTHOS

Myth
is mouth

as is
the Ruined
Tower

This is the secret
of forbidden
love

NIGHT SONG

1.
I can't write my way to health
or Wisdom (realization)

it's all I can do
to write my Way
at all.
And yet

I *do* write my way
past the need for justice

past
pain

stay with the life of the mind
while bony hands pluck me
                    out of my
                    sheepskin
                    bed

2.
Imaginary
toadstools
w/ real
doors in them.

3.
We got by
when Mercury hung
in the west

got by
w/ other planets

now gone missing

LUGHNASA

for Sheppard

As soon as the sun goes down
the air turns cold.
A raven flies thru the twilight
calling his mate.

FIELD OF FLOWERS

"Before I am lost
hell will open like a rose
for the dead to pass"

Space is a lotus

everything issues fr the Black
& nothing is
anything but
itself — measured
thus —

Chrysanthemum

&

The Rose of Paradiso wd be
closer to the truth of it if it showed

each petal
an entire rose
another
Paradiso
un'altra *Beatrice,*

vedi?

each petal
New Orleans
Jerusalem
Carcassonne
Alexandria
Kabul
nothing other than itself
Paris
Damascus
Golgonooza
Venezia
tutti gli altri

Baghdad
city of magic
city
of dreams
measured thus

towers of benediction
facing out
toward
gold & turquoise seas
indigo / skies
white foam
of galaxies
breaking on no shore

Space is a Lotus

blossom in its roots
everything issues

in the cities of man the
City of Benediction

that never was
except in our minds' eye

the black chrysanthemum

waiting
on ghetto roofs
black helicopters
alien insect saviors

from a different
civilization

who move sand
move delta mud like we
moved mountains
once

BUT NOWHERE IN ANY OF THESE
WORLDS
IS THERE ANYTHING
FIXED
OR STATIONARY
—Giordano Bruno

as the green earth
broke into blossom
broke
the spheres
broke open to
manifold
(Indra's net
jellyroll of
implicate order
homing OUT)

as the earth blossomed it
simultaneously
shattered
broken heart
patent & vulnerable
the end now
always
in sight
last deeds
of the marching
Saints
foot soldiers barricading invisible
angels

aluminum bars

stun guns

soon to be laced

w / morning glory

hyacinthos

gone to earth

those are pearls

"all to be changed"

MADHYAMAKA

I want to stop looking
at the burning woman
the eyes
of the starving child

NOLA a flower
from a warmer
world age.
Extinct
as mammoths
or forests of giant ferns

"tree" they said is actual
"forest" exists in the mind

music

each *being*
real but *city*
a fabrication

here's where "your philosophy"
falls apart, there's always
more than the sum

not fabrication
but fabric

connective tissue

SEVERAL THEORIES OF FORGETTING

by Lance Olsen & Davis Schneiderman

These are the dreams we had.

These are the dreams we sometimes should have had.

Perhaps they weren't dreams.

Perhaps they should have been.

The planets weren't planets, in any case. They were Zeppelins. Jupiter with an undercarriage, gaseous Venus piloted by monocled Germans. Think of Saturn, ringed, flying across the nighttime Atlantic, a banshee moan from a muted foghorn; the moons of Jupiter an entire luminous fleet, ambient silver scintillations.

The sun, of course, comes in at the end and burns everything up.

You see what I mean.

For the sake of us.

You, or a disturbing stranger who looked precisely like you, squatted behind a little puppet theatre, using naked Barbie dolls to explain something to me.

I couldn't understand what you were trying to say, so I began signaling you back to this effect by making gestures with the fingers on my right hand.

Digital semaphores.

You looked puzzled, then angry—the Barbie dolls were smooth and tan—and then you huffed and closed the curtains. The show ceased.

When I approached the apparatus to talk to you, you weren't there.

I don't believe you ever had been.

Attendees at an unnamed conference kept disappearing into your hotel room, and, upon emerging, wearing personalized tattoos.

No, "tattoos": swirling words you had written, less tattoos than mystical talismans, ashen, smoldering markers of some other dimensional alterity.

I never saw you, or the room's interior, but I did have a conversation with your adult son, whom you don't, in fact, possess. He looked nothing like you, but I knew who he was. He had close-cropped (but not buzzed) hair and was in his early twenties. We rode down together on the elevator, staring at the red emergency button.

He spoke of you and your wife with an indeterminate, dreamy intelligence, as if he had perhaps imagined you both by chance. Everything he said about you seemed beside the point, like he was talking about people he had only heard rumors about.

His name, I believe, was a word that sounded something like *cloudage.*

While we were seeing each other. Or just after. Those dreams.

You would think we might have been more imaginative.

Be that as it may, this one: the time has come to amputate my mother's left leg. I wish it weren't already that late, but I take some small solace that such a moment happens to everyone.

We are in a dark cement basement with wood paneling. My father helps by sitting on my mother's chest, holding her down, weeping. He has begun to shrink, and is already no larger than a small chimp.

She's *dead*, he is whispering, weeping, head lowered. She's *dead.*

But of course she's not.

He's already shrunk to nothing.

A song plays in slow reversal, like polychromatic fishing lures snapping back to the sun, the shore, your rusty tackle box. Lucifer speaks like Jimmy Stewart in *Harvey*, telling me about your Greek grandfather who, having come to America in the late teens, returns to Greece at the end of the 1920s to find a wife. On the island of Lemnos, he emerges from the boat. Whiskers overgrown in the salty air, he snaps his fingers and two porters unload a large crate from steerage. He snaps again, and inside: a wind-up Victrola playing the devil's lullaby. Snap. The potential wives come running.

Water nymphs.

That one again.

Every night for a week.

Next you are sitting in your publisher's office, ingested by a large plush chair, even though to the best of your knowledge you are not a writer. You don't like books. There are too many words in each of them. You like words to be few. I am standing in the doorway, but no one seems to notice. That's the way you want it. Your publisher turns out to be a very fat man with a very furry beard and wire-rimmed spectacles. He is wearing red lipstick meticulously applied.

Your manuscript is brilliant, he says, thumbing through it in his lap. Masterful. If a little long.

A bit long? you ask.

By about three hundred pages. Yeah.

You explain that it's only three-hundred-fifty pages *in toto*. He asks if you are willing to trim. Say yes, you know, and he would be happy to publish the expurgated edition. You don't think. You say absolutely.

He taps its pages into alignment and slides the whole to you across his desk.

You take the first page off the top of the stack, ball it up, and chew it. Swallow. Reach for the next. Chew. Swallow.

Your publisher looks on this ordeal with real pride.

From the doorway, I share parts of this emotion.

You suspect what happens next may take some time.

You are falling through the night. Predictably. That dream. You don't know where you were before you began falling. You don't know how long this has been going on. You're faintly embarrassed by the unoriginality of your situation. Then you find yourself lying in an immense treeless field. This too, is predictable. You hear voices. Rain smashes down around you. Yawn. You open your eyes to see a squad of Nazi soldiers—of course—closing in on you, flashlights sweeping, firing machine guns. The bullets begin hitting you. They don't hurt so much as frighten.

It is only when the soldiers are fifteen or twenty feet away that you see they're all wearing translucent masks of either your mother's or father's face, or mine.

A month after we broke up, you phoned to share this dream with me.

You slut, I said, kidding, sort of.

I wore a mask of your face.

And then there's the one—

No, wait. That was something else.

In the dream, you are me. Not the me who writes, but the me before writing. The me before thinking.

This seems unclear, so I ask you to explain to me, as me, what you mean. You offer an example, in my body. You raise my left arm and with an effortless flourish, snap each knuckle like a bullwhip. A shiver runs down whosever body. Goosebumps. We smile.

You offer yourself to me, in my body, a fantastic *auto-da-fe*. We writhe on the dream bed, my hand your hand, touching us until we explode outside the body and back into our separate persons.

The next day we meet in our usual spot. The waiter brings us our usual steaming coffee mugs just as we reach the usual table.

We sit there, mesmerized by each other's arms.

Inside our baby's silent cry sits a primitive biped, perched on her larynx like a gargoyle. Our baby dreams hard, eyelids fluttering like molecular engines powering some transubstantiation of this world into another. Her blue body shivers and prunes as she paddles below the frozen surface of a fjord, drops inside a submerged cave. At the bottom of the world, where even the white translucence of protozoa gives way to dark empty water, she stops flailing her arms. Her legs go still. Here it is. She has found it.

You dream that you no longer dream. Not that you no longer recall your dreams. Not that you simply cannot access the glary sheen of the gas lamp across shadowed cobblestone streets while you move, in an oversized waistcoat, across the quay. Not that your vision smudges. Not that you are flying, were flying.

Not that you dream, but cannot recall your dreams.

Not that. Not that at all.

Your mother is in a hospital bed, this time dying of chemo. She is also pregnant, her belly beach-ball big, in labor. This is proving problematic, but the doctors refuse her request for a C-section.

It's simply too dangerous, given the disease, they explain.

There is, though, an experimental treatment she may qualify for. It involves a puppet theater, a zeppelin, an orange peel.

Is that one yours or mine?

I want to say you always dream of my mother, dream words into my mouth, and by dream and I want to say I mean something else, like how in some the heart grows old first.

It turns out you are on a crowded train from the suburbs into the city. It turns out this is where you work. It turns out you're not one hundred percent sure what your job is, but you remain cautiously optimistic that this will become clear, given enough time. You have an itch on the top of your head, the part they call *the crown*, where age begins shedding first. You scratch, then absentmindedly examine your fingernails. They are covered with brain tissue: glisteny, fatty, translucent, with a close-up bitter scent, like something that might lounge sightless on the seafloor. Your eyes dart up, checking to see who might have noticed. White fluid is running down the back of your neck, moistening your collar.

Be honest: this isn't going so well, is it?

Your nightmare: you dream you can't fall asleep. You dream you are lying in your bed, staring up at the ceiling, for hours on end. The gritty charcoal darkness. The nondescript ceiling that is, in fact, not unlike the nondescript ceiling above your undreamed bumpy bed.

The orange peels with a sickening squish. This is what you used to call foreshadowing. The segments juice between your teeth. Tiny veins catch on the lip of your tongue. Your stomach hurts—mine—it doesn't matter. This orange peel, against the counter, becomes a continent unmoored from the world, some bright Lemuria. Call it *rising action*. You always loved that phrase, for some reason. Use it. Go ahead. I don't mind. In any case, you collect the peels from the counter and run to the toilet, naked, tripping over a porno magazine you've never seen before (maybe one time) crunched beneath the stainless steel foot-pedal garbage can.

The toilet lid lifts with a sticky *thwip* and you can feel the inflation of the soft bowl cover—once white, now stained yellow from years of etc.

A bladder opens its lungs to the world and you inhale deeply and etc.

We can do better, I think.

And then I think: no we can't.

A brief dream: clergymen with three-cornered hats and hog faces.

See what I mean.

While you dreamed that orange again, maybe I was dreaming the dream where I am pushing you down a drizzly suburban street in let us call it a hospital bed. I need to get you to the emergency room mostly, if not exclusively, because you aren't you anymore. I awoke to discover you had turned into someone else entirely during the night. I don't mean that metaphorically. Different features. Different haircut. Different clothes. Some of them mine. You are as unnerved as I. Only then I land us on a cul-de-sac. I turn up the nearest sidewalk, wheel you into the hallway of the house at the end. A family sits on a long faded blue couch in the living room, watching a television show in which you—the old you—play a minor part. You are there and then you aren't there. You are there and then you are tuning a guitar. Rubbing you fingers together. Fingering some sort of naked doll. I want to call it a sitcom. No, a dramedy. No, one of those police-chase things. There are perhaps eight family members, perhaps ten, all ages, all sizes, on said couch. Some look like criminals, if we could agree on what criminals look like. While I think exactly this, nothing more or less, you shove back the covers, hop off the bed, and join them, taking the place of the youngest teenager cramped between the blah mother and the blah father. They make room. You settle in. The displaced teenager stands there a second, figuring, then strolls by you, down the hallway, thinks again and hops unceremoniously onto the hospital bed. He looks up to me, eyes pleading for us to move on.

From what I can tell, the television show fails to end.

I have a deep suspicion you made up the dreams you swear you didn't make up.

I never mentioned anything to you one way or another. Neither did you. I believe this points to vague character flaws in us both.

If we still lived together, I am confident I would continue to fail to share this with you.

You dream the sun is expanding. Through your window, you look at it whitening the sky. A windy fall day.

The leaves crackling, then igniting.

A squirrel. The carpet. You.

No, not you.

This.

Now.

PICTOPOESY

by Joel Lipman

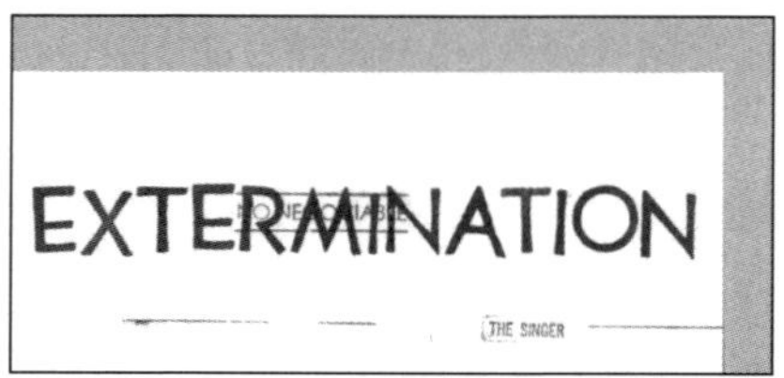

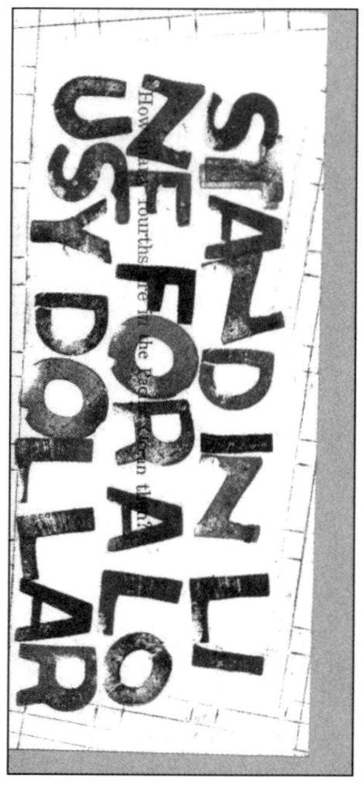

(Continued on p. 131)

NEW WORKS

by Bill Berkson

TED BERRIGAN

"I only have two rules, really: always finish what I start, and never below a certain level."
—T.B.

"Dear Bill, You are having Pronoun Trouble, and I mean only Pronoun Trouble."

*

In the minor leagues of art, there is no forgiveness.

*

Cowboy Leprechaun
Fisticuff Senator
Midnight Scholar
Clown Arriviste

"Shut yer trap"

*

"Poetry should be something real – not just an interesting lie to tell your mother."

*

Hand-lettered Lefty

"Now I see why your poems always seem
to be on the moon
trying to get back
to Earth."

*

In the lap of the gods
snack wrappers crinkling down the aisles

"30,000 feet above sea level
He never rode in a plane"

POETRY AND SLEEP

All this
None of that

It matters here
Dear illusory remains

We remember not what's
Allowed but simply given

Antiseptic disputes over
Pure clove of youth

LADY AIR

The meaning of guitar practice
Slips between pine needles
A bird that thin
To the tune of "Start Me Up"

Rubrics of screen porch and firefly
Embolden the effort

All words are prophetic
Bare the thread, swallow the cloud
Reflected glory drives off
Leaving the original in demand

Repeat after me

EXOGENY

is when the swimming pool casts its poetry
from the side of your mouth
blue yacht rhythms pop at the flickering
bauble on the wrist of personable
divinity you guessed the flavor
made the rounds

now actively, now not at all
whoever lies down by that edge has the fever

DECAL

Coffee to go in either hand
Shady exit down the spa steps
Indentured tulip morning engine zenith

A butterfly speeds off
Weary of these flats
Where palm trees pose and the children push

Macabre distinctions all told
Tragic as a near miss for indifference sake
The moonlit frigate sequestered on a reef

She'll have the silver taken at one of her lengths
Turn the air to proper then
Make mine magnolia

LANDSCAPE WITH CALM

for Nick Dorsky

Pronouns raise the day in kind
    search me a face

To patch
    in phrasebooks

"Say 'Ah'"
    "Arghhh"

Refresher will keep makes
    cold turn coils

For vacant-headed air
    more robes described in wheels

Brains seek crawl space
    scramble

Through towns of name
    to look

Shake out
    the instant nerve

Periphery lifts a clumplike orb
    whence whole

Eras of suds
    come elucidated

Light breath across the windshield
    the first raindrop scuttles

Mild of eye still goes by word
of mouth of world

Your call to hold it
completely initiated culmination's not

A childhood wish
interminably avoided

But coming and going
the sight of things

That intermittence contains us
to the last blink

So much for options
direct address

A panoply of perfect
luster bouncing

News off the moon
all consummate matter welcome

Once motions cross at fatal lip
no other step will double do it

IN OUR TIME

Miss Manners

"Thank you."
"No problem."
And if there was a problem?
Pas de quoi.
Je vous en prie!
Prego.
Bitte.
You're welcome.
My pleasure!

The Big Store

The population has grown, increased:
the world has more people
-- more rich people
and many, many more poor people
because that's the way it is,
and so we know
how many more people
there must be.

THE DOPE ON BILL BERKSON

Bill Berkson, poet, art critic, and presence, has two books that we haven't yet studied, *The Sweet Singer of Modernism & Other Art Writings, 1985-2003* (Qua Books, 2003), and a beautiful collaboration with the artist Colter Jacobsen, called *Bill* (Gallery 16 Editions, 2008). Among his many works that we have read, if not sufficiently studied, are *Fugue State* (poems) Cambridge, MA: Zoland Books; *Our Friends Will Pass Among You Silently* (poems), Woodacre, CA: Owl Press; *Sudden Address: Selected Lectures 1981-2006*, Brooklyn: Cuneiform Press; *What's Your Idea of a Good Time?* (with Bernadette Meyer), Berkeley: Tuumba Press.

This last cornucopia of Bill Berkson books came to us thanks to an appearance by the poet himself in New Orleans. Berkson gave a spectacular reading at the Gold Mine Saloon, that demonstrated a number of things: 1. the Gold Mine has created a sophisticated audience that can hear with the best of them at St. Marks' Poetry Project or at Intersection; 2. so well can this audience hear, the usually reticent poet bounced forth for an encore, like other astonished greats this year, Ron Padgett, for example; 3. there is a new way to read Berkson after hearing him.

I have been a long-time reader and appreciator of the intelligence, music, care, and humor of Bill Berkson's poetry, but this reading gave me new access to his verse. There was always something of a mythical aura about Berkson, the collaborator of Frank O'Hara and one of the chiefs of the New York School whose friends included painters as well as poets. The cover of *Fugue State* is by Yvonne Jacquette, that of *Sudden Address* by Philip Guston. *Sudden Address*, a selection of essays on poetry and painting is a manual for hearing and seeing the works of Philip Guston, Alex Katz, Yvonne Jacquette, Frank O'Hara, John Ashbery, and Kenneth Koch, among many others. Berkson's constellation of friendships led to profound and useful reflections on their work and constitute, in this book and elsewhere in his work, a solid bridge between the two arts and an enlightening guide to the New York School and, in effect, to the modern proposals of these arts in the last half of the 20th century. The delightful *What's Your Idea of a Good Time?* is a spacious and joyful collaboration on the title question.

In his dedication to me, Bill asks, "Dear André, What's the worst thing you've ever done? (see p 51) Love, Bill." On p. 51, we find a number of the worst things Bill Berkson has ever done, including: "I was incredibly mean to Frank O'Hara one time: I shouted at him for liking the sound of his own voice too much." Now, anyone who's ever been told that by a dear one has permission to smile, and that smile will get wider as the implications begin to dawn: Frank O'Hara, the poet who was all about voice is being told by his friend to pipe down. How alive is that? And how much more alive does that make Frank O'Hara, dead now four plus decades? It's not the worst thing Bill has ever done (this bit is No.2 of the worst things), but it's one with cosmic reverb. Berkson's own poetry is subtle and demonstratively abstract in the manner of, let's say, DeKooning: it has an imagistic hardness and lushness that sweeps aside whatever you might have been thinking before you got to: "as if pins were/ to be pushed dimly/ inches downward from/ a manila star." And speaking of pins, the name is Andrei, Bill, not André, it's Romanian not French. That's rude, but not the worst thing I've ever done. Berkson is one of our greatest contemporaries, and shouting at him over a lost letter and a misplaced accent makes me feel great. The new way of reading Berkson's poetry that hearing him granted me was to regain an intimacy with the work. When distance intervenes, years or miles, one tends to lose one's ear. Hearing him was a joy, and the grace of reconnecting to the page a real jolt & gift. (ac)

MASK OF PROSERPINA

by Alice Notley

THE WINDOW TO FLY THROUGH

In the old city drifting rain followed me
as I thought along the morning
Are we waiting till we end,
just a few centenary days she
might be thinking,
This is a form, but who will know of it

I've been here for ages your poet the
same one you've always regarded across
the page in the back of your throat.
Broken yellow geraniums on the
sidewalk where there's usually puke. It's
pouring; the liquified flowers look like paint

At the time of our fall "I
wouldn't be shocked to find out that by
2100 most things were destroyed"
Can't remember
that scientist's name. Who will?

So that in the heart of it the black sleeves
are forgotten, on. You only wear them
You are late with your project of portraying
the life of a flower.

. . .

I have to get up and she keeps being there,
tries to make me go shopping for clothes.
I say no and hate the situation, I don't
want her there or disfiguring anger

. . .

near the cameo lake that time was
scarcely 20 years old I arrived and
was told an established character might
speak, one of two women admitted
that year.
I always need to remember which
window is hers when I fly back.
I slept with a number of men
at that time

I hope that she won't watch
I never stain
it never rains

. . .

you find where
you aren't vulnerable

you must do this now

the window I leave myself through.

I have to stay out after door's locked
in order to find him tonight so I
must memorize her window.

yes I know he's dead
I know it in this dimension

we'll get in a car and drive north, or south
south if someone's just died
north if I must be submissive

These are memories but not of what happened.

TALKING TO THE BODIES

Now, I fly out to others

I go there talking to the bodies
there isn't going to be a human
plan after future point which clings to me
fly back and forth instant arc

though I go I've always returned
to morning, and sometimes I fly only to meet
you, one you, as if a long time ago
when we met. Can't untangle love can be felt
for any human body lying there in the
further field near the flat gray -- who
will perceive gray -- lake. Don't bring this
big downer I'll bring what I want

. . .

I fall in love with another future corpse
I send him anonymous collages
Get me to the airport I know I'm
leaving. He's
showing the men at colleges these dangerous
collages, who can have made them so
I tell him I did,
he was analysing these gold
and distributed red word for wasn't really
beautiful unless broken now. I
can't know intact man will love
you broken
In world formulaic you have hoped no
it is dissolution for words to go and the
flower our species gold . . . I've sent
you even more of them pink and black with
a fireplace look I must have known these
didn't need to last; what will last you
formidable fire burning up the tell
him it's from me this page; I wanted
you to have it when I left. I'd done
something similar to another man
I was a danger but only where that
idea danger existed not now in the future

THE MASK OF PROSERPINA

To agony a famine I said but that
was futile, she doesn't want it
She takes the silver cup away and gives
me the mask of Proserpina. You
will have power in no world except that of the dead
Go back up to Spring for your
purse; you must always return for
your money when red flowers bloom
Of course or else I wouldn't have a life

Proserpina repeats
I cross over
I do cross over

the she who pains, that whore. because
I have to attend. if I didn't there
wouldn't be a life; if I couldn't tell
you you'd offended me there wouldn't
be a life so listen to how I was cheated
by you, but soon

The conflagration of your times took
place while I put on the mask
of Proserpina to rule the future dead black
dress whose songs are one bridge on which
to walk across

there was no breath there not about
breathing. When I go and there is no she
Fly over the bodies and over them
isn't there another empty all-field
isn't there a way to do this without being
Proserpina

That is, I took the mask home

. . .

She was slender and had been given a black
bandanna
twisted but can you break the lake?
I still knew always and will when there is
only one I the same as none

you can always find some more bodies twisted

Now the mask is kept in a cardboard box
at home for
when he's done
when he's done with what he thinks is saving her

Do you know bending,
breaking and twisting. The torturer,

They confronted me
with my poems.
too intricate and golden for that face of mine
a mask no one can look at

Mask of ancient aversion
You all gathered to meet her asking for a
display
of power. if I am a configuration
there is nothing but power

To be a configuration can I leave
or reconfigure

can any handful of words stand in for me

. . .

I am about to leave a dorm
room to meet some men or him. There's
a girl in bed and I'm going to slip out
the window next to her bed I try to
remember if there's a curfew think
yes as if from the last time I was
in college. So it is too late: you'll have
to slip out she says
Hoping to remember which window
is hers when I come back
when I have reconfigured

OBSERVING THE OLD FORMS

when the tourists guarded by guns
observing the old forms in the ancient
city in their shorts come the year
thousands die in a few weeks doesn't
feel unnatural for we were there just
being there. what did I need to know
of war and climate, thrilling words to mate
near the shores of castigation but
who would want to listen?
I myself the historian was there, in
that city at that time. The poet rather
But the stories are immaterial for the
flower is wilting and no story remains
except that of the flower's death
This is the story I'm telling
but on the side of the feral angels
another being flies

child's class remember assignment to
draw flowers as they age due yesterday I thought
it was myself but it was everything. They
are casting inside the drawn ring light
it on fire burn it all up for money burn the
whole damn world up for money throw it
away wasn't this your privilege. He
will take you where he pleases and you will
go; he will destroy us and you will go with
him.

. . .

Some where someone is left and has found a
manuscript. I was dreaming of it dreamed
human the whole thing and when the
vultures pecked the dream out of my
brain they were dead. No one has to care
about it you can just read a novel this year.

And it was a quartz eye that was mine
as I flew
Flew over the dead lake in the copper
landscape
So I couldn't see the colors

Sex was dreamed for the sake of nothing
Nothing ate it.
This is natural light it beats down
there is no stain
aren't you too hot
I'm not really anywhere. Nothing
ate it
can I have a new mask. flame
behind black mask of Proserpina
flying

TELL ME EARRING

you will always in the flesh for you
want that river, getting next to his skin I
lied I wanted you, I wanted you to
tell me earring. We won't
have to really because the club is pro-
cessed and I know you have to belong to it
you have to in their eyes as if there
were still animals of which you too: but
we are no longer they. having evolved from
mammal into taint a body of conceit but
I would be next to yours for a brief haul
to shadow shadows to float in.

She
has left the room of the others you must
display for don't really know her someone
asks me of where she's gone if it would be a
good place to watch the end of the world
Anyplace would be wouldn't it I say

if you had seen yourself you would know she
says, that you are that mask, through which
to watch. Stand close to the cut-glass tower
in our town. This beautiful drawing
of donkeys is all us; I still have a desk
and mail and keys; colored ribbons hang
by my door, red blue and green, to entice
you to come in. Come in. I said to him.

. . .

I found this beautiful language at the
end what will I do
Say it to your diamond ear you are
here. The two bodies were sensual not
being young contained a swollen throng
of knowledge contradicting holes
I have mouth for your call, speaking to
this close landscape I lose my balance
I don't fall. Would you fall for this
close landscape wanted to make love
reproducing nothing

TORTURE WAS THE FIRST THING

I thought he was going to come to me five
thousand miles. because we could have had that
instead; or you can say he won't let her go
"he won't let her go on tour" the tower
repainted gold to watch them come down
invading the climate. Then you can torture whoever
you wish reason recalling songs as if you loved someone
keep doing this maddening thing until
you come to the beginning of the world the scourer-god
but to go back
but to fly back
go up
and god will tell you he was given nothing
nothing to love, but that was you. I am inventing my own heart
the rat in the closet: nothing pains me
I singly derive every letter to incise into you
surely no one would do that crying out as
someone else thrust hot words in

. . .

you mustn't leave me even if the world ends
you have to believe there's no self but the phrase,
"there's no self" even if
even if it ends do I want you
when the rocks melt with the sun

I have ripped the plaster of paris off my torso
impersonally yours,

dirty with the furniture close together. it was their
black wood-burning stove, there is no wood left
in the world
I want to fly overhead hear me calling but
I have to stay the girl.
Go in and complain that you will never be
cold again, because you are Proserpina
And he is being fired
I want to leave but I have to iron
because this world dull heavy and hot
has been given to me by god the scourer whom
everyone worships, fearful of rats by
now the only other animals left. do this to
me, please do. I am doing it again and
again.

where would I find any rest except in
a word when all words are gone

I flew to you beg cheerfully
there are so many ways to humiliate one
until she sings
so many masks
the rat crawls

I put on the mask
stare through to reconfigure
as air or fire as word

I wanted you all across my times and so was
of them
but different
as to flight since you
couldn't created disunity and couldn't fly
when even a rat could disappear into itself

THE PLIANT PAGE

I am a worthless fellow creature
I stand for the absolute individuality
of each one
I know that you are unique; this is
what poetry has shown me
that any poet however terrible
will not make a poem
like another one's. It is impossible
and so, the self exists.
if you know this you will not kill

I can see and love it
covered with words which are essence
plasmic and transparent

. . .

Had I broken the solar system the voice said
in lightless dream the world was seen
impressed by fingers becomes pliant

and the rectangular solid of the poem
bent
squeezed gently into an unanticipatible mass
(for what future)

they argue in a car where else
one in favor of the art work, which is known
useful and priced -- so regular
and one in favor of the pliant page he is
scornful of the art work

will you wait for me
I have to put on my mask to have form
they pressed quiescence
blood from my arm that wore wildflowers yesterday
semi-straight brown hair wants to
read books, scrolls and fans, old
manuscripts
when first I came to these shores
the sun was perceived as gold empress and light our gift
splits the line to bend for clarity's edges are
soft I stain in public vowed to show how
you ironed light like a sheet rushes
back former model trails collapse

. . .

we will do it till something kills us
and reconfigure in another part of the
universe
is that to be pointless
read this then one says it is more precise
than you are though one sees you

I don't believe you will help me. You want me to
want what you say is

On the manuscript moving in the wash
a mark brown and blackened
may be the form of mask holds me to
your eye
if you look to violate me through my
treaty mask
you may find there is no face, only eyes

it wasn't the treaty of union it was the acceptance of separation
I have left you but am waiting
still can't follow
being my own fair sun
as in any dream where you might see anything, unlit

BREAK-IN

whatever you break you can have
if you break the weather it will enter you
and be all yours; you will have to live it

But I am not you
what have you stolen from me

I've been broken into, what's left but
the business goes on
And I am the one who goes out
to find a locksmith barefoot, barefoot
must change the lock
I must keep you out
of me.

You are hiding this darkness from yourself,
not a word. Men work in the store part for money

I flew to find a future voice
 Could we take it as a fact, says a voice,
that that text is not hidden

. . .

   I need your tongue should you take it
maybe you should the thief
 says. The text spread out for its past to
read Oh can you hear
   the device of darkness there is no such thing
                    as darkness
I will make you mine though I am a
dead end doctor.
 It is the doctor when you beg keep still
in the jewel breeze for wind strangely
blows must keep it out. broke in
 someone stole me for their own. Now you can't
find your war
   I take it this text is here. Yes it's here now
 there is no one, not even war

break in. ruby lock don't let it
for I am generous he is the thief
he is the present thief I keep changing my
  locks
the darkness of the longest white hair
  will not keep him out of there.

that the text is not hidden but you can't
  read it
Change my locks my private Angola

. . .

it didn't matter what country it was my love so

if I reconfigure
   the wind scouring me flatly
because of the money made in any year
 the text has no year
it can't make you happy. Just because
   you left like that

after taking as many diamonds as you
could define as yours
I remember waiting for you because you
seemed bigger
Now I have reconfigured as the large dark
mask, circling the planet, looking for
spring.

I remember I wasn't supposed
to be there when you came. I
had broken in but you were
bigger; everyone said to leave. I
myself want to be bigger is that a
valid desire not for a woman and now
I'm bigger even than you as far as
known masks are concerned.

every time I flew out to meet him it was
a disaster
I did all the calling
calling you to break in there will be no
you but disaster

. . .

I haven't read the whole I know
it bends you to it
what is written
I bring it back word by word

oh you thought you'd penetrated the skill of
not remembering. though you ex-
pected to be remembered

SHE

and someone's searching me. I was on my way to
a shopping center in the last
world long print cotton skirt. who will remember
long string of yellow beads; or pinning it on me,
that was she. but *he* wouldn't *bother* to blame me
The shopping ring I mean binding conversation
with staff, you do have a staff, but no
conservation of the place where you are, called
dead looking woman.
Then she turns up says she's found some

dress and she
chose it, deserves it; I'm holding her place
in department store line several women gone ahead
of me and now I'm angry, tell her to pay for
everything herself I go out other woman standing
there. I implore her to Help me, give me something
Who wears the
golden chains now; I don't even know how

to wear a thing, Do you have your mask on
How would I know

how would I even know when I have my mask on?

when you're disconnecting
Butchie seems to live here all encrusted
where I'm first now in the future

one drop of painful
sexual urine
you can have that
when you learn how.

. . .

the person on the side of the angels was on
her own side. if you want to reproduce that
side, it's too late. even if it's the only side you like
But there's no practical side, now
the only thing left in is beauty. I want it
badly, I walk toward what used to be love
you will hit me if I do this. who? she will
I've had her for too long to continue to
want her. Yes I became a poet, instead of
becoming her, as the mask sank into my face
carving its outlines there. And the care I had was not to
propitiate you; you can go. Other woman goes

is she the only one you've rejected, was I
born for that
but nothing matters now I keep
forgetting

I am watching the mass of interpretation
sink into desert land leaving a black burned
cerrate oval, scorched rock

EIGHT POEMS IN BLACK, AFTER GOYA

by Jerome Rothenberg

two women watch
a man his hand
under his cloak
or in his pants the act
that causes one
to grin, the other
wryly looking on
as in a dream

•

a procession of
old whores & madams
toothless
bearing fardels
& a gallant
from a former time
lined up along the base
of a grey mountain
holy crones
& well-laced fathers
of the inquisition

•

A PILGRIMAGE FOR SAN INSIDRO

who but the dead
can scream so
with their eyes rolled back
their mouths
like black holes
whom a blind man leads
strikes a guitar
& to his left
two men in black
two women in half-white
without a face

•

Saturn
devouring his sons
whites of his eyes
as brilliant as
the red blood flowing
from the severed
neck
blood on his hands
his penis hot
& throbbing

•

man fighting man
with cudgels
drawing blood
a stream of red
across his face
& sinking
ever deeper
into the mud

•

a poor dog
hidden in the brown
& yellow mud
that could be clouds
– the way they suffer
without sound –

•

THE WITCHES SABBATH (1)

Satan as a great
goat black
& holding court
before a ring
of men & women,
too deformed
from watching
the small figure
crouching
covered with
white shroud,
& at the edge
a young boy,
almost cut
from sight
the only
gentle soul,
whose screaming
mother hollers
at the assembled
crones

•

THE WITCHES SABBATH (2)

red more brilliant
than her eyes,
the blanket set across
her mouth,
poor doll & witch,
& yet the eyes
are turning backwards
in her head,
the one who flies with her,

a rock between
his teeth, a tongue
made stone,
the yellow wind
spiking his hair,
who has no choice
but points a finger
at a hill in space,
a city on a hill,
that vanishes.
Nothing has changed
since then,
try as we will,
nor will it please you,
friend & father,
the ragged soldiers
aiming guns,
the line of pilgrims,
barely seen,
circling the lonely fell,
the old witch
like a sibyl
arisen from your dream
ready to tell it all.

THE ANTHOLOGY AS A MANIFESTO & AS AN EPIC INCLUDING POETRY, or THE GRADUAL MAKING OF POEMS FOR THE MILLENNIUM

by Jerome Rothenberg

I would like to go back over my own relationship to anthologies & to contrast it to a general discomfort I have with anthologies as such, before entering into a discussion (however it falls out) of this anthology or of "the anthology as an epic poem and/or a manifesto." In 1979 I had done five anthologies, the most recent of which (*A Big Jewish Book*) had been published by Doubleday the year before. It was with relation to this that Charles Bernstein, who was then editing the important (poets') journal of poetics, L=A=N=G=U=A=G=E, asked me to write a piece on my own work &/or "on anthologies." I began it with a quote from Gertrude Stein about the new & the old, since the anthologies I had then made were a conjunction of modernist poems with ancient or culturally distant works of near-poetry that I wanted (in Robert Duncan's words) to "bring into their comparisons." What Stein wrote (words that I've quoted a number of times since, as I have a way of doing with quotations) was: "As it is old it is new and as it is new it is old, but now we have come to be in our own way which is a completely different way."

With that as an epigraph, what I tried to do was to distinguish two, at least two, kinds of anthologies (a point that seemed to me self-evident): those that deceive me/us by a false sense of closure & authority, as over against those that I had hoped to do with regard to the past & those still more rare & useful ones that opened up & thereby changed the present. (Both of the latter I took, rightly or wrongly, as instances of a single impulse.) The canonical anthologies we all know as the great conservatizing force in our literature(s), against which—as artists of an avant-garde—many of us have had to struggle. As gatherings of acceptable/accepted poets their conservatizing thrust is evident; as gatherings of contemporary poets it is to rein in or exclude those moves that challenge too overtly the boundaries of form & meaning or that call into question the boundaries (genre boundaries) of poetry itself.

The other possibility of anthologies is to use the form as a kind of manifesto-assemblage: to present, to bring to light, or to create works that have been excluded or that collectively present a challenge to the dominant system-makers or to the world at large. In my time the great American work of this kind was Donald Allen's (1960) *New American Poetry* (replete with its appended section of poetic statements/manifestos), but also LaMonte Young & Jackson Mac Low's *An Anthology* (as a manifesto of the 1950s/60s Fluxus movement) and Emmett Williams' *An Anthology of Concrete Poetry* as a first summary & presentation of the movement of that name. Still earlier works were Pound's Imagiste gathering & later *Active Anthology* or (better yet) Louis Zukofsky's "Objectivists" anthology of the early 1930s (a prime example, that, of the construction of a movement through a book—& little else by way of publication).

From these I sensed the possibility of the anthology as (1) a manifesto; (2) a way of laying out an active poetics—by example & by commentary; & (3) a grand assemblage: a kind of art form in its own right. My first anthology, *Technicians of the Sacred,* grew from premises (theory) within experimental modernism, rather than from critical authority situated outside it—what Tristan Tzara implies in his (1918) postmodern divergence, that "Dada is . . . not a modern school . . . [nor] a reaction against the schools of today . . . [but] more in the nature of an almost Buddhist religion of indifference." Beginning in that general area I was able to explore an open-ended range of deep cultures, of culturally embedded poetries & related language works, many of them subsumed as poetry by resemblance to contemporary work & in that comparison also opening the range & giving a new depth to the experimentally modern. So too I used the last quarter of the book for a section of commentaries that not only gave some ethnographic context to the traditional pieces but allowed the entry & comparison (for better or worse) of a number of more contemporary works (an early revival of Gertrude Stein & a mix of new & old voices, of the modern & the postmodern: André Breton, Diane Wakoski, Tristan Tzara, Gary Snyder, Anne Waldman, Allen Ginsberg, Ian Hamilton Finlay, Simon Ortiz, Hannah Weiner). This was of course the hidden (secret) heart of the collection, what made it (I hope) not a book of antiquities or orientalisms or primitivisms, but a manifesto for our time: each commentary a pointed statement of a way of poetry long overlooked.

All of the anthologies I've assembled since then—by myself or with others—have shared in this; or, to use a key word of the 1960s European Situationists, who helped so much in the development of a strikingly "appropriative" postmodernism, they have been a *détournement* (a turning or a twist) on the structures & presumptions of those fixed anthologies that continue (like the darkness) to surround us.* After claiming it as a right, I later found that I had gotten leverage to continue & to expand this work & (with Pierre Joris as a powerful co-worker) to construct an assemblage of the twentieth-century that would bring together (on a global scale) works entirely of this time that had been (the greater part of them at least) too often kept beyond the pale or, if present, had been kept from those comparisons, those co-existences that were so real to our generation of poets throughout the world. In that sense I would bow also to those many others who have been our companions, even forerunners in this attempt: cultural hunters & gatherers (or, simply, formal & experiential innovators), who recognized that the common work cut across boundaries; that alliances & strategies were international, intercultural, in scope; that it was possible to seek wholeness

*In *Poems for the Millennium* such détournements extend to the overblown subtitle (*The University of California Book of Modern & Postmodern Poetry*), the Board of Advisors (largely themselves experimental poets), the quasi-scholarly commentaries, & the various other accoutrements & paraphernalia of the official book.

or completeness while knowing that we never would achieve it; that the explorations & discoveries of a new poetry & art were precisely what made the attempt at wholeness possible.

That work, which Pierre Joris and I called *Poems for the Millennium,* is now complete and its two volumes and 1600 pages (some twelve years in the making) are generally available. The first volume ("from fin-de-siècle to Negritude") covers the century up to the second world war and is the first such gathering to put the avant-gardes and movements of that time into a place of principal consideration. With that in mind we were able to devote whole sections to six of those movements (Futurism, Dada, Expressionism, Surrealism, the American "Objectivists," and the African & Caribbean Negritude poets) and to draw on individual voices from a still wider range of languages and cultures. And we were able to show too—if it needed showing—that multiculturalism and avantgardism were not incompatible but historically, though not inevitably, related. Our last section, in that sense, was devoted to ethnopoetic explorations from throughout the century.

The gathering—in so far as it smacked of "anthology" in the ordinary sense—was replete with problematics & anxieties. This intensified of course with the second volume, which moved us into the (almost) present; moved us, literally, into a time & poetry in which we shared. The tough thing here—and we knew it from the start—was that as an an anthology (& I mean a largely contemporary anthology) it had to be a flawed book—a compendium of absences as well as presences; & we knew too that there was no way that it would not be read as an anthology in that sense. For me, though—and I'm sure this holds for Pierre as well—it was conceived, like other gatherings of mine or his, as something else: an assemblage or pulling together of poems & people & ideas about poetry (& much else) in the words of others and in our own words. That imago—that representation of where we've been and what we've lived through—is something in fact that I would stand by—like any poem. (It's also why we've allowed ourselves to end the book—as epic poem replete with histories & voices—with two poems of our own.)

What is missing from that gathering exists in the still greater gathering we carry with us—as a mental, a spiritual, construct. It is in this sense that every one of us has his or her anthology, that every one of us, given the opportunity, could bring it into some kind of form or structure in the outer world. At the end of a joint interview with Chris Funkhouser, following the publication of volume one, Pierre suggested that as far as future projects went, the two volumes were (for us at least) "the anthology to end all anthologies." To which I added that the only anthology still left to do was "an anthology of everything." In saying that I suppose there was an echo of Mallarmé's intuition that "everything in the world exists in order to be put into a book." By that measure, of course, Mallarmé continues to be a guardian angel for the work—one of those who led us into the domain of the impossible, which is really where we want to be.

Talk first presented at the Modern Language Association December 30, 1995, modified for presentation at the Boston Alternative Poetry Conference July 18, 1998.

TWO FROM KANADA

by Kane X. Faucher

ELECTION COVERAGE

Sweater-wearing Neocon Stephen Harper wins minority gov't in 2006.
Harper belches on about "young criminals" and "more police state!"
Harper receives monogrammed cowboy boots from his pal, Bush.
Harper follows Bush policies to the letter, including lowering taxes while spending more on military.
Due to election fatigue, Liberals abstain from voting down Harper's legislation to prevent a dissolution of parliament that would send us back (again) to the polls.
Liberal leader Stephane Dion is about as charismatic and well spoken as John Kerry with a stutter and a stroke.
Harper proposes and signs into law that there will be no election until 2009. (remember this)
Harper proposes enormous cuts to art, calls artists a "niche market of gala-attending debutantes" that does not represent "ordinary Canadians."
Harper whines that parliament is "dysfunctional" (read: all the other parties disagree with his fascist ideas).
Harper breaks own law to call snap election in greedy power grab for more power in the hopes of forming a majority gov't. We pay 300 million to go into an election only for NOTHING TO CHANGE. Harper gets same minority gov't.
Kane drinks vodka and yells at TV screen, openly bemoaning how many people who can't tie their own shoelaces seem to be able to vote. Kane drinks more vodka and thinks of his own power bid; starts blaming poor opposition leadership, paces around yelling into phones and smoking. Kane is too restless to sleep. Wife urges him to sleep it off on the couch.

SERFS UP ON FACEBOOK: GOGOL-CAPITALISM

Like most of us who have been politely press-ganged into the online breach of Facebook, I have a digital portrait. And, like most of my ilk in that flaked and canned real, I, too, used to use Facebook as something to satsify my Shadenfreude in seeing how ugly and fat my high school ex-girlfriends became, obsessing over every little bowel movement status change minutiae of my contemporaries, and accepting friend requests from former co-workers I could never tolerate in real life. But all of that has changed: I am now a Facebookie and I have Gogol to thank.

We can forget Google entirely when it comes to potential personal market gains since, like any origin of bizarrely good ideas, we ought rather to appeal to a crazy Russian who starved himself to death. It is a credo I have lived by, and one that has mysteriously worked to my frequent benefit.

Facebook's bubblegum conviviality in its virtual la-la land kitsch utopia does not, despite the raft of over-eager enthusiasts and starry-eyed media theorists, present us with anything altogether new. In fact, Facebook has had its precedent already firmly set by Gogol's *Dead Souls*. Apart from the close affinity between *Dead Souls* and Dante's *Divine Comedy*, Chichikov could be considered, under certain aspects, a probable mascot for Facebook and its attempt to achieve the dream of a total global social network, and a means by which social cachet may be increased by the organization and accumulation of "friends." Could Chichikov's single-minded endeavour to increase his virtual wealth symbolically express the goal and totality of a social network at its highest end efficiency? Could *Dead Souls* actually be a primer on the successes and failures of various social networking strategies, including Facebook? Well, serf's up, kiddies; let's consider the act of face-trading, the trading of faces like bubblegum cards, and go right for the raw throat of a proposed experiment.

What we propose is a social networking experiment that would push such networking to a commodifying extreme. Facebook accounts are already reductive and artificial representations, based mostly on idealized ego projections in a public space. There are several facebookers who recognize the inherent irony of making oneself public, and have undertaken to creating accounts for B-rated actors, dead poets, dotty emperors, or even inanimate objects. I myself have thus far collected over a thousand such "fakebook" friends having tucked into my greedy rucksack of social capital the entire canon of Western scribes, gaggles of Roman officiocrats, swathes of popcorn-era rubber monsters, leagues of pub-crawling philosophers, a murder of crowing politicians, and a junk trove of sitcom characters. From ET to Mr. T, Countess Bathory to Count Chokula, Jehovah to Jiffy Wipes, the Jackson Five to the number five, I have amassed a veritable historical conglomeration of figures both failed and fabulous.

Collecting "friends" is not limited to people like me with one foot in Russian imperialism, nor is the act of foisting upon the public realm a fake account the sole enterprise of cheeky cyber-satirists. The CIA ritually create sham pro-Jihadist accounts that function as a terrorist honeypot (of course, instead of endless posted pics of undergrads debauching at parties, we are probably privy to devotional icons of gun-toting Imams reposing at home with their Korans and Kalshnikovs). But before we jackknife unnecessarily into the penury of combative ideologies, let's return to our precocious Gogol.

As we know, *Dead Souls* follows a modest entrepreneur by the name of Chichikov who cleverly has discovered a loophole. Since the census only came around every five years, landowners were still obliged to pay a head tax on each of their serfs, even if some were deceased, until the censor came around to confirm their death. Chichikov's shrewd plan is to effectively offer these landowners a bailout package and assume ownership of the dead property so that he can use it as asset leverage at the bank and secure a robust mortgage on land (the US government should be so lucky in its collection of toxic debts). Gogol's *Dead Souls* is a double portraiture: a portrait landscape of provincialist Russia and a series of portraits based on archetypal characters that form and represent a tight and caricatured typology. It would be misleading to limit the title of the novel to merely the main character Chichikov's buyout of uncounted serfs when in fact, it is the landowners that dot the narrative landscape that can be called spiritually dead. Facebook, on the other hand, is also a double portraiture: the superego graft of so many Dorian Grey faces within the immense folds and knotted clusters of a social networking landscape.

Dead Souls is not so much geared toward the pageantry of peasantry as some Soviet-era critics have suggested through the myopic lens of revisionism and communist romanticism. It is more the tale of a crafty capitalist trying to artificially inflate his capital assets so that he can borrow more heavily from the bank. More importantly, the book was one of Gogol's first attempts at penning an arabesque. There can be no better representation of a social network than that of an arabesque with all its ornamental intertwining, multitudinous connections, and confusing knots. Crafting an arabesque can be as time-consuming and meticulous as building a social network. Arabesques, if done well, can be objects of supreme aesthetic beauty; done poorly, they resemble spaghetti dinner after two bottles of Scotch.

The dream of cataloguing every soul has been with us since the Roman census, the *Domesday Book*, the Nazi's *Deutschekartei*, and every secret and not-so-secret service on earth. Facebook seems to incline toward such an encylopaedic task, and so some of its members think it absolutely exclusionary to eschew the induction of more members on some silly prejudice of extending membership to solely those who are living or non-fictional. And so, like a Borgesian aleph, Facebook's population continues to swell with the living and the dead. However, Facebook's terms of service make it abundantly clear that the practice of adding these benighted and deceased souls constitutes misrepresentation, and many are the monitors who sweep through and summarily execute these fakebook accounts. Sadly, these puritanical torquemadas neglect to consider the enduring irony of such a staunch diktat when the majority of "legitimate" users are among the most flagrant in their own misrepresentation. As well, there are those fake accounts that are perhaps indirectly protected by populism insofar as campy or contemporary celebrities are targeted for deletion while noteworthy philosophers, writers, visual artists, and Victorian politicians can remain safely off the radar of the Facebook account liquidators.

In Facebook, quantity takes precedence over quality of connections. But one of the aspects of Facebook that continually goes understated is how users will freely surrender all their personal and proprietary information under the seemingly innocuous auspices of "being social." In such cases, the demands of ego-dissemination trumps the prudence of privacy. Based on the information users so profligately splash on their profiles, Facebook is able to sell said information to slavering marketers to better direct advertising. Given the amount of market-preferential information people were giving up, including their geographical location, age, religious denomination, gender, and so forth, Facebook realized early it was riding a cash cow.

According to social network analysis, a social network is measured by degrees of connection. Each actor or node has an assignable degree according to the number of real and possible connections he or she has, and their placement within the network. Facebook, for the most part, has an infinite potential for connectivity, although it can only proceed incrementally. With over 100 million users, a user can potentially try to add each and every one, the limitations mostly being placed by the number that will accept or reject a friend request. Interestingly, Facebook places its own restrictions on how many connections one is allowed to have. Every account is only permitted a maximum of 5000 friends. Facebook feels that, perhaps, having 5001 friends is a tad excessive. There are real-world reasons for this limit that have nothing to do with some ulterior motive on Facebook's behalf to regulate the maxima of friendships, but they are not particularly interesting. What we retain here is that each account has a potential connectivity degree factor of 5000. This means with one account I can only connect to 0.005 % of all Facebook users. Pity.

However, having 5000 "friends" is not too shabby if taken in another way, a Gogolian way. In tapping out at 5000 souls, I would have a sizable base of potential assets. Even if the account is fake, there is still a live person operating it, and so even the fakebook accounts are viable in their salability. If each account gives some information as to the person's location, gender, preferences, religion, political orientation, relationship status, and can have posted notes and photos at the ready for my consumption, what would prevent me from selling my account—with its full instead of limited access to a market base of 5000 users—to some corporation's marketing department? Evil? Perhaps. Gogolian? Definitely. In a telling statement by Ina O'Murchu, John G. Breslin, and Stefan Decker in their article, "Online Social and Business Networking Communities," the authors put it baldly: "The aggregation of information gathered in the user profiles makes them extremely valuable and collectable." Collectable, indeed. A collection implies the possible completion of a set, and this consumer-based libidinal urge is perhaps, in Freudian manner, an attempt to recollect oneself.

The easiest and quickest way to acquire 5000 Facebook souls is to scour the site for any fictional or deceased personage that has an account. Such accounts are actually created to gain mass attention, and so will more than likely indiscriminately accept a friend request, whereas a random and real nobody-user may not. One could criticize the quality of such connections, especially since these are fake accounts, but we are talking quantity here. Would the moneylenders question Chichikov on the vitality and labour skills of his serfs? Not at all. It doesn't matter if the accounts sold to a marketer are mostly bogus any more than if the number of serfs reported by Chichikov to his lender were karked—death and fiction are just details. As long as it looks viable on paper, the numbers have some at least minimal basis in reality, that's all that matters. It is as easy as approaching a corporation of your choice and saying, "I have the intimate market preference information on 5000 people for sale."

Chichikov's plan of buying up a slew of dead names on landowners' registers at a significantly reduced sum still required funds. To acquire them via the Facebookie method is virtually free. In fact, one could set up several accounts and while away the time adding ever more souls to one's collection, sell them at a tidy premium, and do it all over again. Facebook acts as the intermediary and directs advertising to the user, whereas under the more Gogolian plan, a user would give full non-intermediary access to users without having to go through Facebook. Does this violate Facebook's terms of service? Most likely. If you are the kind of person who is willing to sell out your friends to advertising harassment, does that matter? Most likely not. If you like the idea but have a nagging conscience, just repose in the safety of it being "satirical" or ironic.

Gogol employs the *Skaz*, or oral history, in his style. As Fredric Jameson writes in *The Prisonhouse of Language*, "It is not because Gogol wishes to present a certain type of content that he appropriates to himself the style of the *skaz*; he wishes to speak in a certain kind of voice, and, given that initial starting point, then looks around for the appropriate material." In like fashion, being a Facebookie does require getting familiar with the online vernacular. The "eSkaz" (which is perhaps reminiscent in both sound and type to "ersatz") is the common linguistic currency for Facebooking.

Facebook is not so much a rhizome of connections, or some revolutionary hypertelic superconductor; it is still a highly regulated structural phenomenon that parodies capitalist practices. It is human nature thrust into a virtual milieu with all the trappings of hierarchical arrangement, possibilities for greed, and a medium to air out our dirty egos like the shameless exhibitionist monkeys we still are. Gogol already had humanity pegged in *Dead Souls*, and it made no difference if the system in which it was situated was imperialist or capitalist; if the apes had clubs or laptops and guns; or if there was a king or a gang of thuggish morons running the whole social circus. Facebook is what we choose to make it, yes, but the options are limited by the inherent limitations of our desires. If you choose to rack up friends like trading cards in order to make a tidy profit in the end, that's your bag. If you choose to construct meaningful and lasting relationships via Facebook, all the power to you. But let us not condemn Facebook for utilizing all the petty, corporate-crony tactics it does since we are just as capable to doing so as well. It is by way of Gogol that we put this thing to bed: "It is no use to blame the looking glass if your face[book] is awry."

FOUR HINDI POETS

translated from Hindi
and introduced by Arlene Zide

SHRIKANT VERMA

Shrikant Verma (1931-86), a poet from a small town in Madhya Pradesh, Central India, had a career in both journalism and politics. He was General Secretary of the then-ruling Congress Party and rose further to become the speech writer for the late Indian Prime Minister Indira Gandhi. While he wielded considerable clout in such power circles, his poetry was haunted by self-doubt and paradox. He worked in genres such as poetry, the short story, the essay, and published twenty-five volumes in all. He was awarded almost all major literary awards during his short life time. *Magadh*, his book of poems named for the fabled ancient Indian city, remains one of the groundbreaking works in contemporary Hindi poetry. To express his deeply ironic take on the contemporary political and social scene, *Magadh* employed familiar historical and mythic places—many of which have not actually disappeared, but have simply evolved into vastly changed modern towns or cities, but still possess immense resonance in the Indian psyche.

CORPSE IN KASHI

Have you seen Kashi
where the road a corpse goes down
is the same road it comes back on?

So what about corpses?
Corpses come
Corpses go.

Just ask
whose corpse is this?
Is it Rohitashva's?
No No
every corpse can't be Rohitashva.

If it is
we'll know it from far away
If not from a distance
then from close by
and if not from up close
then it can't be Rohitashva.
And even if it were
what does it matter?

Friends
you've seen Kashi*
you know the road the corpse goes down
is the road it comes back on.

---

*Kashi is the ancient name for Benares (Varanasi) on the Ganges.

whose corpse is this?

All you did was just this —
gave way
and asked —

Whoever's it was,
Whoever's it wasn't
did it matter?

[co-translated with Gagan Gill]

MATHURA'S WAILING

Can you hear the wailing of Mathura?

This is what happens —

Mathura wails
when Mathura is nowhere
Mathura! Mathura!

Mathura is just one example
Take Avanti
Listen carefully —

Did you hear it?
It groans again and again?
Avanti! Avanti!

Didn't I just say it?
people moan on and on
about Mathura
not being Mathura
about Avanti
not being Avanti.

Maybe we'll get used to the wailing
over cities
no longer there
But —
Mathura and Avanti
are not memories

And even if they were
who will believe
Mathura and Avanti
are only memories?

[co-translated with Gagan Gill]

THE HORSEMAN

The horseman
rides to Kalinga*
Is he the same one who comes back?

What do people say?
Victor!
or Murderer!?

Do brides
welcome him?

or does he wander
aimlessly
What happens?

Horseman,
Where does this road go?

[co-translated with Gagan Gill]

AMRITA BHARATI

b. 1937 Najibabad, U.P. She holds an MA and Ph.D in Sanskrit from Benares Hindu University. She has lived in the Aurobindo Ashram in Pondicherry and is presently at Vivekanand Kendra Yoga Research Foundation, Bangalore. Amrita Bharati is a unique, idiosyncratic poet belonging to no particular "school" or movement in Hindi poetry, who says of herself: "There is very little of the world in my poems. The reason for this is not unfamiliarity with the world, not a sense of detachment nor a lack of sensitivity, but rather, a wait for some real purpose between me and this world. Poetry doesn't have any independent truth—my truth is the truth of my poetry and it can always be discovered in a new way. . . The distance between me and my poetry is. . . minimal, almost nil. . . when your vision is turned outward, then it presents things as and where they are. But when it's turned inwards, it begins to see such things as they ought to be—man, society, the world, relationships, even things within their essential nature."

DIFFERENCE

I was a true mustard seed
He, just a huge mountain of lies

He talked for hours
about gunpowder
so when I handed him a match
he backed up
like an unbroken mule.

---

*Kalinga is the ancient name for what is roughly the state of Orissa in modern India. It is one of the places where Ashoka planted his stelae.

Running through the mustard fields, that mountain
turned into

first, a camel
then, a jackal
then, just an empty thought.

[co-translated with Aruna Sitesh]

HE, THE ADIVASI (TRIBAL)

He was only he
atop the raised hunter's blind
they all
were either inside
the cage
or were sneaking up from behind
his hiked up shoulders

It was only he
on top of that hunters' machan
a tiger
looking for a tiger.

[co-translated with Gagan Gill;
previously published in The Little Magazine, 2006*]*

GAGAN GILL

b. 1959 , Delhi, Gagan Gill's "existential" work is widely recognized both in India and in translation. Quintessentially "contemporary," it often uses devices such as soundplay and repetition intertwined with contemporary themes of alienation, covert sorrow, and impermanence. Considered one of the outstanding poets of her generation, she had a successful career as a journalist, but chose to give up the journalist to the poet in her in order to secure the "long periods of silence in her everyday life" which she considered necessary to remain "truly connected to words." She has published four collections of poetry and two volumes of prose: her first collection, *Ek din lautegi larki* (One Day She'll Return, the Girl), focuses on the gamut of female experience (but also includes epigrams and verses about political events); the poems of *Andhere me Buddha* (The Buddha in Darkness) are variations on the theme of sorrow in human existence; her third volume, *Yah akanksha samay nahin* (This Is Not the Time for Desire), is dedicated to the enigma of desire; the songs of her fourth collection, *Thapak thapak dil thapak thapak* (Thump Thump Heart, Thump Thump), rely on sound and images, rather than narratives, to crystallize suffering as the one constant in the impermanence of human existence. Those who are familiar with Buddhism will see the reflections of the Buddha's four noble truths in much of Gagan's writing. She writes about pain without sentimentality or overt emotion. Her intensely psychological poems are understated, deceptively simple, filled with repetition, yet extremely well- crafted. She combines stark images with expressiveness composed of gaps and silences, with absences and even disruption which sometimes goes beyond language. Gagan Gill was a visiting writer at Iowa International Writing Program in 1990 and a Nieman Fellow for Journalism at Harvard University in 1992-3. She lives in New Delhi.

NEARING THE HANGMAN'S NOOSE

Nearing the hangman's noose
What is the first man thinking?
He's thinking couldn't he
have been the last man?

Walking towards the rope
suddenly, he realizes freedom
from the terror of death.

Suddenly, free of attachment and illusion
Just one thing stays with him –
his envy –
of the last man.
Infinite envy.

Reaching the end
he turns for the first time
and looks
at the last man
as though assuring with his own end
this last man's end as well.
In this helpless dark instant
what else could he have done?

[co-translated with Madhu B. Josh]

GOD IS WATCHING YOU

God is watching you in a dream this time. In one of his eyes it's you and in the other, her. How you parted—God's watching it all.

This is a frightening dream. In it are several trenches. Many darknesses from before earth's beginnings. They were not even there then, God thinks in his dream and watches you tumbling down.

You yourself are half inside God's dream, half outside, up to your neck drowning in water. Above it, drowning in thirst. God's watching you in his dream and a tear is forming in his eye.

What is this dream which never comes to an end? What is this tear flowing over all the earth?

[co-translated with the poet]

FRIENDS

> "Whoever has no house now, will never have one
> Whoever is alone, will stay alone."
> —Rilke

-1-

The wind
is soaking up
their sounds of laughter
The wind is soaking up
their secrets, their sorrows.

At this very minute, blood gushes out
Once they part,
they will be left shadows
of themselves.

This is the hour of God.

He knows
what is going to happen to them
once they go away.

Leaving all his work behind
He's come
to watch them all.

At this moment
all of them move
like puppets
dangling from the magic hand of God.

God has finally arrived
It's bad news.

This is the hour of God

They
the orphans
of God.

Never let yourself dream of friendship...
Friendship is a miracle. Simone Weil

-2-

God won't ever come to them
again

The world will become
immense
full of continents and oceans

They'll roll all over it
all of them
like balls
There'll be no path
anywhere
to their friends' houses.

He'll forget, God
to map the longitudes and latitudes
Their parts of the world
won't be anywhere.

The earth will be outside
the Time of God.

They'll roll
over the cruelest
surface of the universe.

[co-translated with the poet]

RAJEE SETH

Rajee Seth, b. 1935, Nowshehra, Cantt. (NWF, now in Pakistan) has been writing for over thirty years and has won several major awards for literature in India. She holds degrees in literature, comparative religion and philosophy. She is a renowned short-story writer, novelist, poet and essayist. Her literary work includes all genres of literature. Her work has been translated into several languages. Her works have become the subject of several post-graduate and doctoral dissertations and are now prescribed in many post-graduate-level courses in universities in India and the U.S. She was awarded an International Institute of Advanced Studies Fellowship in Simla, India and was a member of the Advisory Board of the National Academy of Letters for five years. She currently lives in New Delhi, India.

TERROR

You don't see the hands
which clasp the axe
What you see
is the glint
off the blade
held high in the air.

You see just the necks
unprepared
innocent
Which moment when
where
will the axe-blade
fall?

[co-translated with Aruna Sitesh]

THE BRAIN (OF A FASCIST) & THE HEART (OF A JEW): MIRCEA ELIADE & MIHAIL SEBASTIAN (CHRONICLE OF A BROKEN FRIENDSHIP)

by Andrei Oisteanu

IN SEBASTIAN'S DEFENSE (1934-1935)

In 1934, following the publication of the novel *De două mii de ani...,* [For Two Thousand Years] with the infamous foreword signed by Nae Ionescu, Mircea Eliade publicly defended his friend Sebastian, polemizing with their common mentor. Among other things, in his article Eliade raised against the "certitude of Jewish damnation," and Nae Ionescu's opinion that Jews had irremediably lost their access to redemption. *Extra Ecclesiam nulla salus*, in Origen's formulation. To judge this way, wrote Eliade, meant "to intervene in God's free will," who "could redeem anyone, by any means." In two other articles, Eliade continued this controversy with theologian Gheorghe Racoveanu, fellow contributor to Cuvântul and a friend of both Eliade and Sebastian. There are "certain Jews," Eliade would nevertheless admit, who "are Devil's sons." These Jews "shall not find redemption."

Eliade's jump to the public defense of his friend Sebastian was obviously a laudable and courageous act. Sebastian fully appreciated it. In august 1934 he wrote him the following in a letter: "Your answer [to Racoveanu's article], dear Mircea, [was] excellent. You could not put it better. I am deeply sorry you were dragged into this mess, in a way because of me." This was the time when Sebastian was attacked from all directions, from the right and from the left, by the legionnaires and by the communists, by friends and by enemies, by Romanians and by Jews. For the Romanian P. Nicanor, for

instance, "[Sebastian's] intellectual profile is primarily hooliganic", while for the Jew Isaac Ludo, Sebastian is a "dramatic bone rodent," a "lowlife," a "scoundrel," a "dejection of the Jewish ghetto." In short, Sebastian was too Jewish for the Romanian nationalists and too Romanian for the Jewish nationalists.

But Mircea Eliade approached the issue of Judeophobia from a somewhat too "cold," too "technical," strictly theological perspective. Consciously or not, he largely ignored the political perspective (not to speak of the moral one) of anti-Semitism. At that moment, in the mid '30s, the Romanian (and European) Jews were in need of physical, not metaphysical, salvation. They needed redemption on the earth, while still living, rather than in heavens, after death. In fact, Sebastian himself sarcastically amended this theological controversy in his book *Cum am devenit huligan* [How I Became a Hooligan]: "I do not claim any right to have a say in this debate [between Eliade and Racoveanu], which, moreover, in its depth, is profoundly and totally indifferent to me. I have a vague impression that after my death I shall not be judged by Mr. Racoveanu's texts. And if I am wrong, let God's will prevail."

Still, Sebastian fully appreciated the fact that his friend Eliade was one of the few who jumped to his defense. On the cover page of his volume *Cum am devenit huligan,* Sebastian inserted a dedication showing his gratitude: "To Mircea, who did not let me despair while standing the miseries related here [in the book]—which will only survive, if they do, because he had a say—the most beautiful (Mihai, 1935)."

SLIDING TOWARDS THE FAR RIGHT. FIRST SIGNS (1935-1936)

In the fall of 1935, Sebastian started to notice "that he [Mircea] is sliding ever more clearly to the right." "When we are alone together we understand each other reasonably well. In public, however, his right-wing position becomes extreme and categorical. He said one simply shocking thing to me, with a kind of direct aggressiveness: 'All great creators are on the right.' Just like that" (27 November 1935).

Everything still seemed remediable. Sebastian's decision was firm – to avoid at any cost the breaking up of their friendship. He was convinced he had even found the appropriate strategy: "I shan't allow such discussions to cast the slightest shadow over my affection for him. In the future I shall try to avoid «political arguments» with him" (27 November 1935).

In less than a year, however, this strategy would be proven wrong. Or in any case, impossible to apply: "I should like to eliminate any political reference from our discussions. But is that possible? Street life impinges on us whether we like it or not, and in the most trivial reflection I can feel the breach widening between us." (25 September 1936).

In the fall of 1936, the "painful political arguments" between the two friends seemed harder and harder to avoid, leading to "irreparable discords" (see 25 September 1936, 18 October 1936 etc.). "He [Mircea Eliade] is a man of the right, with everything that implies—Sebastian noted in his journal on 25 September 1936. In Abyssinia he was on the side of Italy. In Spain, on the side of Franco. Here [in Romania] he is for Codreanu. He just makes an effort—how awkwardly?—to cover this up, at least when he is with me. But sometimes he can't stop himself and then he starts shouting, as he did yesterday. . . Will I lose Mircea for no more reason than that? Can I forget everything about him that is exceptional, his generosity, his vital strength, his humanity, his affectionate disposition, all that is youthful, childlike, and sincere in him? I don't know. I feel awkward silences between us which only half shroud the explanations we avoid, because we each probably feel them. And I keep having more and more disillusions, not least because he is able to work comfortably with the anti-Semitic Vremea, as if there were nothing untoward about it." Nevertheless, Sebastian concluded on a still hopeful tone: "I shall do everything possible to keep him [Mircea]" (25 September 1936).

Mihail Sebastian didn't know what to choose between the intellectual value of his friends and colleagues and the moral one. He didn't know whether to adopt a position of political tolerance or of ethical intransigence. For example, his reaction of embarrassement at the contact with Dragoş Protopopescu, who became "an Iron Guardist" (journalist at Porunca Vremii and coeditor at Buna Vestire), is symptomatic: "There should be—and it's not the first time I say this to myself—there should be more intransigence, more rigidity even, in my life, notes Sebastian in his diary. I am too 'souple'—and I utter this word with a touch of scorn for everything in me is too accommodating" (15 June 1936).

BETWEEN LOVE AND HATE (1937-1939)

But things developed speedily. By 1937-39, Sebastian's friends were disturbed by his presence. They would change the subject or keep silent whenever Sebastian stepped into the room. Only their dog Joyce—uninfected by the microbe—"shouted with joy" at his sight. "Only Joyce reminded me of the time when I felt somehow at home in that house" (30 August 1938). "Our friendship is rapidly breaking up," Sebastian noted in his diary about his relationship with Eliade. "We don't see each other for days at a time—and when we do, we no longer have anything to say" (25 March 1937). Subjects were changed in Sebastian's presence. At times, in despair, Sebastian himself would ask Eliade to change the subject. "But is friendship possible under such circumstances?" he wrote in his journal on 4 April 1937.

In December 1937, Sebastian felt he was about to lose all his friends, including "the closest friend of all, Mircea" (19 December 1937). Indeed, it was then, a few days before the elections of 20 December 1937, that the famous ill-fated text "Why I Believe in the Victory of the Legionary Movement," signed by Eliade appeared in the far right publication *Buna Vestire*. "Can the Romanian people end its days… wasted by poverty and syphilis, invaded by Jews and torn apart by foreigners…?" Sebastian transcribed, stupefied, in his journal, a fragment from the text published by Eliade (17 December 1937). The long and vivid political disputes they had along 1937 did not manage to clarify things. "He's neither a charlatan nor a madman. He's just naive. But there are such catastrophic forms of naiveté," concluded Sebastian (2 March 1937).

The two friends' encounters were rarer and rarer, until they ceased completely: "It's nearly two months since I last saw Mircea," wrote Sebastian in his journal at the beginning of 1938. "Should I let things unravel by themselves? Should I wrap it all up with a final explanation? I feel such revulsion that I would prefer us both to stop speaking once and for all. I have nothing to ask him, and he certainly has nothing to say to me. On the other hand, our friendship lasted for years, and perhaps I owed it one harsh hour of parting" (13 January 1938).

When, half a year later, they eventually met again, Sebastian did not know how to manage his relation with Eliade. Out of control, his feelings oscillated between sympathy and antipathy, between love and hate. "Dinner at Mircea's on Sunday evening. It was a long time since I had seen him. He's unchanged. I looked at him and listened with great curiosity to what he said. The gestures I had forgotten, his nervous volubility, a thousand things thrown together—always congenial, straight-forward, captivating. It's hard not to be fond of him. But I have so much to say to him about Cuvântul, about the Iron Guard, about himself and his unforgivable compromises. There can be no excuse for the way he caved in politically. I had decided not to mince my words with him. In any case, there's not much left to mince. Even if we meet again like this, our friendship is at an end" (12 April 1938).

The relation between the two friends was oscillating. Sebastian constantly felt he was loosing Eliade and then finding him again. On 6 March 1939, he offered to Nina and Mircea Eliade, as a gift, his new volume *Corespondența lui Marcel Proust* [Marcel Proust's Correspondence], with the following short but meaningful dedication: "To Nina and Mircea, found again." On July 22 of the same year Sebastian joyfully commented in his journal "a meal in a garden restaurant" with Nina and Mircea, where they felt "like in the best times of old." Everything seemed to be mendable.

But, on 1 September 1939, Hitler

waged war. Mircea Eliade was, as Sebastian noted in his journal, "more pro-German than ever, more anti-French and anti-Semitic." "What is happening on the frontier with Bukovina is a scandal—Eliade told Petru Comarnescu—because new waves of Jews are flooding into the country. Rather than a Romania again invaded by kikes, it would be better to have a German protectorate." Eliade was having the same problem as in December 1937, when he had written the text "Why I Believe in the Victory of the Legionary Movement"—an obsession with "the invasion of Romania by kikes." In less than two years, "the closest friend of all, Mircea" (as Sebastian still thought of Eliade in December 1937) was degraded to "my ex-friend Mircea Eliade" (20 September 1939).

"IPHIGENIA, OR THE LEGIONARY SACRIFICE" (1939-1941)

In December 1939, following his liberation from the Miercurea Ciuc camp, Mircea Eliade wrote the play *Iphigenia.* In Eliade's view, king Agamemnon's daughter not only did not oppose her being sacrificed, but even made the eulogy of self-sacrifice, of the offering "for the redemption of the others." She could have avoided the oracular decision (by marrying Achilles), but preferred to "throw herself in the arms of death" ("marry death," as Eliade would put it) instead, to allow the Greek army to leave for the Trojan War. The references to *Legenda Meşterului Manole* [Master Manole's Legend] were obvious in the play: "I shall not be built in—Iphigenia motivated her sacrifice—at the foundation of a grandiose construction, to give it breath and life," but at the foundation of Greek victory over Troy.

The choice of the martial subject and the play's meanings were transparent. "In this tragedy in three parts—notes Alexandra Laignel-Lavastine—one can find all the ideological topics that remained dear to him [Eliade]—particularly the exaltation of sacrifice, and of death for the motherland—skillfully integrated in an a priori dramatic script, with no direct connection to the Romanian and European political actuality. Numerous passages are in fact almost word by word reproductions of the articles devoted by Eliade, in 1937, to the Frankist 'sacrifice' of Ion Moța and Vasile Marin."

The play had its opening night on 12 February 1941, eighteen days after the legionary rebellion. A fragment of Sebastian's journal explains everything: "The premiere of Mircea Eliade's *Iphigenia* at the National Theatre. Of course, I didn't go. It would be impossible for me to show myself at any premiere, let alone at one which (because of the author, the actors, the theme, and the audience) was bound to be a kind of Legionary reunion. I'd have felt I was at a meeting in their 'den'. . . The text is full of allusions and ambiguities (which I already noticed when I read it last year. . . The symbol does strike me as rather crude: the play might be called 'Iphigenia, or the Legionary Sacrifice.' Now, after five months of being at the helm and three days of revolt, after so much killing, arson and pillage, you can't say it is not relevant" (12 February 1941). About one month later, Sebastian eventually went to see the play. His comments in the journal were less radical. Still, he noted "only here and there were there annoying Legionary allusions" (6 March 1941).

It has been said that at the time Mihail Sebastian was particularly sensitive, suspicious and subjective. He was, supposedly, an obsessed man who saw "Legionary allusions" everywhere, even where they were not present. But the play's message was "deciphered" in a similar way four decades later in Italy, in an entirely different social, cultural and political context, by the young scholar Ioan

Petru Culianu. Reading the script of *Iphigenia* in 1977, Culianu discovered "with a certain amazement and sadness" his master's association with the ideology of the Legionary Movement. This was an embarrassing "ideological position," which—concluded Culianu—"seems to us today entirely impossible to understand."

Not by chance in 1951, in Argentine, a few Romanian legionnaires published the script of the Iphigenia tragedy. Eliade himself operated several changes. He even added a brief foreword: "I publish with joy, but also with sadness, this play of my youth, which was so loved, at the time of its writing, by my friends Haig Acterian, Mihail Sebastian, Constantin Noica and Emil Cioran." In fact, he dedicated to Haig Acterian and Mihail Sebastian ("two of my best friends") "this text, which we all loved at the dusk of our youth." In 1951, when these lines were being printed, Mihail Sebastian could no longer express his reserve towards such a statement. Nevertheless he admitted in his journal that, feeling embarrassed to tell his friend the truth, he mimed some appreciation of the play's script: "After [reading] *Iphigenia*. . . I use a few admiring declarations to cover my real sense of dissatisfaction" (28 February 1940).

A FAILED ENCOUNTER (1942)

In the summer of 1942 Mircea Eliade came from Lisbon to Bucharest, with a message from Salazar to Antonescu. This was to be his last trip home. Eliade met with his "legionnaire friends" and "all the friends at Criterion," less Mihail Sebastian. Overwhelmed, the latter noted in his journal: "I heard a while ago—but omitted to mention it in this journal (is it becoming so unimportant to me?)—that Mircea Eliade is in Bucharest. He did not try to get a hold of me, of course, or show any sign of life. Once that would have seemed odious to me—even impossible, absurd. Now it seems natural. Like that, things are simpler and clearer. I really no longer have anything at all to say to him or ask him" (23 July 1942). It is significant that Eliade's wife Nina (an old friend of Sebastian's) did not attempt to see him while in Bucharest, either in 1942 or in 1943 (see Sebastian's journal, 27 May 1942).

There have been many speculations as to the reasons for which Eliade avoided Sebastian in the summer of 1942. In the "Mircea Eliade File," published in 1972 in the Israeli journal *Toladot* (no. I, 1972, pp. 21-26), the author advanced a cynical motive: "As a diplomat Mircea Eliade was of course aware of the fate awaiting the Jews. Why, then, should he have seen his ex friend, who was doomed to death?" It was indeed that summer that Ion Antonescu and Gustav Richter (Adolf Eichman's representative in Romania) signed an agreement for the deportation of the Jews to the extermination camps in Poland. Sebastian himself quoted in his journal an article from *Bukarester Tageblat,* which gave an extensive description of the plan to transform Romania into a country free of Jews (Judenfrei) by the fall of 1943 (8 August 1942). But this explanation for Eliade's avoidance of Sebastian is too morbid to be considered true.

In this respect, Eliade had his own motivation. In a letter of 6 June 1972, the Israeli professor Gershom Scholem asked Eliade for explanations in these (and other) regards: "Ever since I met you, I have had no reason to believe that you were an anti-Semite, all the less a leader of anti-Semitism. I consider you a sincere and just man, for whom I have great respect, and that is why I find it natural to ask you to tell me the truth. If there is anything to be said about this, let it be said, and let the atmosphere be cleared of general or specific accusations." Eliade answered Scholem that in Bucharest, in the summer of 1942, he felt he was watched by Gestapo or State Security agents and did not want to direct them towards Sebastian, thus provoking him additional trouble. This was a clumsy attempt to relativize the truth. The same justification of little credibility can be found in Eliade's *Memorii* [Memoirs], also written in the 70s, but not in the journal he kept in Portugal.

In October 1946, while in Paris, Eliade wrote in his journal about his relation with Sebastian and the reason for which he had avoided Sebastian in Bucharest in the summer of 1942: "I shall never find consolation for the fact that I did not see him in August [actually July] 1942, when I went back to Bucharest for a week. I was ashamed, at the time, ashamed of myself—cultural counselor in Lisbon—and of the humiliations he had to stand, because he had been born, and had chosen to remain, Iosif Hechter. Now I am uselessly struggling amidst the irreparable." I think it was only here, in the fragment of his journal quoted above, that Eliade confessed to the truth. In fact, Mircea Eliade felt ashamed and responsible, as a member of a regime that was discriminating and civically annihilating his friend Mihail Sebastian.

POST-MORTEM (1945-1980)

In December 1944, Sebastian made a nostalgic retrospective of his relation with Mircea Eliade in his journal: "Our walks in the mountains, the summers in Breaza, the games in Floria's [Capsali] yard at Strada Nerva Traian; our years of fraternal friendship—and then the years of confusion and growing apart, until it all broke down in hostility and oblivion" (13 December 1944). This was one of the last entries in Sebastian's journal. A few months later, on 29 May 1945, the writer died, run down by a mysterious truck.

Upon hearing of Sebastian's death, Eliade was overwhelmed. Still in Lisbon, he noted in his journal on the very date of 29 May 1945: "The news touches me through its very absurdity. Mihai undoubtedly has lived the life of a dog during these last five years. He escaped the massacres of the January 1941 rebellion, Antonescu's camps, the American bombardments, everything that followed the coup of 23 August. He saw the fall of Hitler's Germany. And he died in a car accident, at 38!... I recall our friendship. In my dreams, [Mihai] was one of the two-three people who would have made Bucharest bearable to me. Even in my legionnaire climax, I felt him close. I gained a lot from his friendship. I counted on this friendship, in a possible attempt to return in Romanian life and culture. And now—he is gone, run down by a car! With him goes another big and very beautiful piece of my youth. I feel even lonelier than before. Most of the people I loved are now on the other side… Good bye, Mihai!"

When, 35 years later, in 1980, he had the chance to meet, in Paris, with Beno, Mihail Sebastian's brother, Mircea Eliade exulted: "Your letter touched me greatly—and it also touched Christinel, who knows all the three of you [the Hechter brothers], from the stories I have told her in the 31 years of our marriage. It is futile to try and tell you more; I would need tens, hundreds of pages. . . I am looking forward to hearing your voice, to listening to you speak about *De două mii de ani*, to finding Mihai again. . . embrace you with old friendship, Mircea."

Paper delivered at the Hebrew University of Jerusalem (24 October 2007) and at UNESCO, Paris (24 November 2007) on the centennial celebration of Mihail Sebastian's birth.

HUNGARIAN VERSE

by Attila József
translated by Ron A. Kalman
and Gabor J. Kalman

OPENING

Lidi's young brother here,
Khan Batu's Budapest relative,
who lived on bread for years
and never owned a royal-blue eiderdown;
for whose poems death
simmers beans in a wooden pot—
hey bourgeois! hey proletarian!—
I, Attila József, am here!

HONEST HEART

I've neither father, nor mother,
nor God, nor country,
nor cradle, nor coffin,
nor mistress, nor kisses.

It's three days since I've eaten,
not morsel, not feast.
But I've twenty years strength,
I'll sell my twenty years.

If there aren't any takers,
I'll sell to the devil.
With an honest heart I'll swindle—steal,
if forced, I'll even kill.

I'll be captured and strung up,
covered by the holy earth,
and deathly grass will grow
on my glorious heart.

THE SEVENTH

If in this world you lay a claim,
let seven births be your aim!
Once be born in a burning home,
once in a flood in an icy storm,
once in a clinic where the mad retreat,
once in a field of bending wheat,
once in a cloister with a hollow ring,
once in a sty with a pigsty stink.
The six cry out, but which is key?
You yourself the seventh be!

If out front stands the enemy,
take seven men for company.
One, who starts his day of rest,
one, whose service is the best,
one, who teaches on a whim,
one, whom they threw in to swim,
one, who's the seed of forestland,
one, whose forebears took a stand,
not enough tripping up and trickery—
you yourself the seventh be!

Should you be seeking a lover,
let seven men pursue her.
One, whose word conveys his heart,
one, who gladly pays his part,
one, who pretends to be the pensive sort,
one, who searches beneath her skirt,
one, who knows where the hooks are,
one, who steps on her scarf—
like flies around meat, buzzing free!
You yourself the seventh be!

If words are jangling in your purse,
seven men should compose your verse.
One, who chisels a city's form,
one, asleep when he was born,
one, in awe of the celestial plain,
one, whom the word calls by name,
one, whose ailing soul revives,
one, who dissects rats alive.

Four scholars and two infantry—
you yourself the seventh be.

And if it all happened as penned,
descend to the grave as seven men.
One, who's rocked by a milky breast,
one, who grabs at a woman's chest,
one, who throws dishes in the trash bin,
one, who helps the poor to win,
one, who works till he's crazy,
one, whom the moon makes lazy;
into the world's tomb you journey!
You yourself the seventh be!

WELCOME FOR THOMAS MANN

Like a tired child who's been bathed and fed
and has now reached his peaceful bed
still begs "Don't go. Tell a story"
(so the dark night won't burst in a hurry),
and while his little heart anxiously beats
he knows not which of two treats
he wants more, the story or that you stay,
so we ask you to tell us a story today.

Tell us like you do, because you are just,
about how in spirit you are joined with us
and of how together with you we stand
who possess concerns worthy of man.
You know well how the poet feels:
tell what's true, not just what's real,
the rays of light that illuminate our mind,
since without each other we're all blind.
As Hans Castorp looked through Madame Chauchat's chest,
let's look through each other and see the best.
Your gentle voice always rises above the clatter—
tell us of beauty and the problems that matter
and lift our hearts from mourning to desire.
As you've heard, poor Kosztolany's life has expired,
and mankind, as did he with his cancerous fate,
struggles with more than one monstrous state;
with dread we wonder how we might be betrayed,
from where will new beastly ideas invade,
is there a poison brewing that soon we will face—
for readings like this, will there still be a place?
The point is, when you speak, we don't fade,
the men remain as men are made,
the women, women, kind and free,
and all of us human, though that's dwindling rapidly . . .
Have a seat. Kindly start to tell your tale.
We will listen, enthralled, all without fail,
and some of us will happily gaze at the sight
of a European amongst the white.

TWO BITTER SONGS

TING-LING

—Hup, hup! Like a joke
slipped in the skirts of peasant girls
you recede beneath the sky, Attila,
the nearly flat-footed punk;
and as your patched butt
adorned with the order of the golden fleece
fades, they stare wide-mouthed: a goat, a bear,
and virgins! old ladies! sunflowers!

MEDALLION

It's useless, I didn't eat yesterday either,
the devil ate instead,
pigs' feet, countries, the future.
And he filled up his belly—

instead of the moons, the suns,
it's my own wild turds that shine,
the seals on my pigsty death!
They're frolicking and making music . . .

THE FORGIVEN SUBMARINE

by Ruxandra Cesereanu & Andrei Codrescu
translated from Romanian by Andrei Codrescu

for some time now I felt the need to dive down to a submerged submarine
to willingly lose myself inside of it not alone but with a drunk fool in tow
to feel clothed in angels bleeding from their lips
to feel my hair electrified by a hurricane a mystery of curls
with a drunken fool in tow we'd make of this a forgiven submarine
but forgiven by whom for chrissakes
by god by animals by creatures stinking of something nameless
I had no idea but I kept humming about this forgiveness stuck in my throat
panting for wanting to lock myself inside this submerged submersible.
&
for sometime now I've been feeling the need for a a co-pilot
because of the original two who'd begun their journey in the submarine
one died in the library under a bookshelf that fell on him
when the submarine hit hard gray matter
the god of boredom walking madly to and fro on the ocean bottom
seized by an appetite for icarus for submarines and depth seekers
the other had barely escaped being devoured and was now dying of hunger
and my need for a wingéd companion was growing unchecked
I had a license to drive in the depths
but since I'd been pacified somewhat by fleshy folds and spirals
I sang the praises of depths only telepathically
depths unentered that my calls reached only superficially
to where thousands of idiots covered the great ocean scribbling
with phosphorescent ink on the foam
but one day the electricity failed and a velvety darkness descended
a deep and nameless forgiveness born of itself.
&
here is the precipice I've been dreaming of
this is what the living diver in me fluttered and whispered for

even if my other was still living in the rubber fossil of *his* hungry other
here it is the journey through the acrid-sweet water tasting of apple peel
here is the abyss the vertigo the funnel of death baring its teeth
here are the sharp salty nails sharpened in the dark
look here is terror looking at herself in the melting mirror a faithful dog
or an unsubtle and a bit brutal lover
here is the hidden wall without a single crack
a fetus in the submerged submarine known also as the forgiven
the two divers were a shook-up pianist
and a nearsighted drunk amerikan beatnik
banding together for dives to greath depths
a pianist with hair from neverland and an amerikan
with transylvanian moustaches sensitized by the imminence of nothingness
his head and armpits shaved one earring in his ear new age aimlessness
gold chains jingling on his ankles setting the ocean foaming
and setting minds to work chewing the cud
ahoy there forgiven submarine
we are diving your way out of submerged and unadorned time.
&
ahoy there submarine you are far very far
happily you are far but already we feel the suffering
of your being wedged within the tight entry
to the ocean's infinite subconscious
we taste each fathom and for each we invent a game
joined by the creatures and flora of the sea who love to bite
and caress our divers' bodies or maybe they want only to understand
the objective of our game which is to kill them with hunger and mystery
to light up their tentacular mouths with the futility of knowing you
pianist with multicolored hair and anklets spirally clinking above
their bulbous eyes
inexplicable remains also your travelling companion
dried in the deserts of arizona
he catches fire from his cuts & burns with a greenish flame.

&

I probably should tell you now
that both pianist and amerikan had ashes for brains
that they were abusers of ecstasy mescaline transgressors
that they did shots of exploding gasoline inside voids
mind-altering gasoline putting out hypnotic snake tongues
from jaws of sharks exploding loudly out of the water
gasoline or maybe a phantom-limousine who knows
delirium is a guardian angel with wings forged from fire
it is the sigh of the exterminator
so the submarine hides in its womb the two delirious voyagers
who could have been elephant-tamers
or holy dwarfs or chalice-bearers with big eyes
but let's return for a moment to the surface of the sea
to splash a bit so we won't forget
that we are simultaneously dead and alive
that we are wounded by the blades of the world
inside our helmets and pilots' goggles.

&

when dead we are dead-tired when alive
unborn energies dance inside us lightning bolts on water
let's return then to the birth-launch of the yet-untested submarine
built in a delirious hour by a people hypnotized
millions of people deposited their hopes inside its body
like butterflies of prayers stuck in a motorized wailing wall
but the insubordinate submarine escaped from under their watch
and was launched downward on a starless night by two thieves
a pianist dressed in a hurry in a sheet of music left on her piano
        along with a yellow rose by a music-lover and fan
and her cohort the beatnik with a flask of mescaline-spiked rum
        and a backpack full of health advice and silver flutes
                holding poison and perfume

before plunging into the depths they both signed something
an identical writ inscribed at different times
(because they were spawn of ages that didn't coincide)
a contract written on a dead man's shirt who floated into port
something stated in large script to the effect that if the abyss swallowed them
their existence would be denied by all even in dreams
and in small-print that one of them will be inside the other outside
for an infinite second without knowing for certain who inside and who out
and that one will be the pilot and the other an angel greedy for the wheel
and that they would be free to change clothes and desires
at the whim of great underwater beasts
and that their powers would be great that they'd be able to elongate
their hands at will and that they could absorb live organs from any creature
terrestrial or angelic and raven feathers onto their skin and the nipples of does
minotaur erections mollusk eyes and also more eyes in their armpits
and an eye in the neck and in their elongated palms
that their ears would be awake and sharpened elegantly
and that they might fold and be folded as the starry foam of the sea
flowed through their stretched toes fanning out
and that the deeper they dived the stronger would manifest the desires
of giant phosphorescent sharks within them and of the unleashed sirens
who followed them in their descent astride the submarine
inside of which the pianist ravaged by lights was now sleeping hard
knowing that in an hour or two or in a sudden huge moment
she'd be wrenched from sleep and hurled into the future
where a new pilot would descend toward her a man
followed by the tracer-bullets of dancers inside bubbles of blood
spilled in the wars of this or that universe class-struggle included
and she might then be compelled to abandon her refuge to swim up
to him losing the submarine submerged the submarine condemned
to an eventual forgiveness a fallen iron tear
a windowless and doorless bullet of light enclosed in its cylindrical essence.
&
I know it sounds incredible but one day the submarine went to confession

forgiveness forgiveness he shrieked like a newborn
because death is surely not a terrifying beast
the pianist and the beatnik knelt down in the coral reef
between pulsing algae and australian fish
the amerikan pulled on his ‘stache as if it was his umbilicus
the pianist twisted her hair like a wounded pharaoh in the hospital
and both were singing a sort of rock ’n roll hallelujah melted by waves
because the sounds pushed through a ceiling of coral
and so they began dancing to the tune of their unusual prayer
and the submarine twirled like a whirling dervish
near to bursting while begging for indulgence
for his long legs starting practically in his neck
his top-model thighs his languid dolphin flesh
hey submarine tell us please now who is going to forgive you
if not the fabulous and vigorous region known as transylvania
hey hey the pianist and the amerikan shouted and wailed
a spiraling kingdom a folded field sheep dogs and the smell of autumn
what do you know *that kingdom* too lived inside the submarine
preserved inside a grail-cup within wormwood-spiced wine
drunk swiftly and alchemically down by the delirious hallucinators
to forget old age and death sterility boredom and ennui
and above all the unquenchable clock with spider-legs from dreams.
&
well if you find yourself by chance or from the practice of poetry
inside a kneeling submarine don’t panic instantly
you have time to ask why is a submarine begging for forgiveness
if it’s only doing its duty in the deepest deeps where only he
and the multiluminous and muscularly rippled sea may enter
and the answer can’t come from what was made only to explore
but from the sea from the waves made sensitive to communication
which hear the reproaches of earthlings issuing from burnt-crisp brains
though they are courageous these earthlings nonetheless
one dressed for bed with her pantheist hair woven tightly in rows
and a velvety tarantula hanging from a golden chain between her breasts

and an entire world ordered bucolically between her praying hands
the other one an unrepentant pantheist with pan tattooed on his belly
and a single track in his one-thought mind: I want to kiss you
both pilots nervous like race horses feeling the approach
of a metaphysical quarrel savable only by a trip to transylvania
transformative changes are stirring in the kneeling submarine.
&
hey on the ocean-bottom transylvania was a riot of forms and colors
a collection of unseen and unheard-of oddities
a squirming of crude green and oil and tree-frog dissolved in cognac
a smooth grand cocktail with the opiate effects of a mega-poppy
this transylvania situated between tactile mollusk-stalks
was a virgin-woman-amazon with feverish nostrils and open pores
equally a young female and an old woman
wanted by all the striped tigers scribbling their appetites and unlucky love
clearly what else but chimera might one look for on the ocean's bottom
or maybe the godhead with its knees in mouth and its cracking skin of void
a striped life a curved death a chlorinated life-death
held tight in a jar on the ocean-bottom who knows why
heyhey let's split from here sub let's go to more complex distant edges.
&
my dear road-buddy and mechanic in your mini stained with motor-oil
last night when you slept I examined the submarine and discovered
that it wasn't built as I'd suspected from a people's hope or a new metal
forged in the alchemical cauldron of an immortal witch's secret project
I discovered to my great dismay that it wasn't even made from the pipe-ash
of misters freud deleuze or magritte or even jules verne or nemo
I examined its silvery fish-scales covering the fine skin underneath
I shaved a patch with my switchblade
and found some worn words on its skin
cut into warm rose marble that was itself a kind of skin
and under this marbled skin I found another soft skin that hardened
when I whispered the worn words I read with the tips of my fingers
and the longer I explored the sub's surface the more certain I became

that it was a phallus stretching on the sea bottom like a guilty love
which had built for itself a sunny villa on shore but at night longed
for its lover from the depths and dreamt the waves
in which she had buried him
and she wanted to plunge into the depths into him to become the seed born
from the desire that first brought her to him and by becoming seed
she might return to find a purity of innocence in the not-yet-born
like a good poetry student with blaga's verses* scribed on her forehead
and I became unaccountably sad because I understood our twisted journey
of marine passions that carried me here was not our common dance
of love inventing luminous worlds in the spirals of the poetry-game
but the whim only of a lovely nymph who needed nonbeing
and forgiveness and the submarine was only a blind innocent phallus trembling
at her side and kneeling contra naturam on knees it didn't have
and he'd have ascended into the sky for her but had no wings
        or hope of them
and I had been brought along solely for my expertise with feathers and glue
I was known for the sturdy wings I'd patched together over the years
and I decided then that you will sleep forever within the submerged sub
you lovely pianist with hair aflame from the passions of living beasts
I'm leaving you one of the two wings I was crafting for our submarine
and I'll ascend unloved and alone to the surface now using the other.
&
oh the pianist was devastated truly like a machine made of twisted fingers
she walked the night sleepless on top of the submarine
and believing it a piano she played chopin and also keith jarrett
a bit of rachmaninov and other pianists who loved being drunk
the amerikan knew that she had the sex of an angel
he knew as well that sewn in her wings were tiny eyes
like sparkly fingernails
he clearly didn't know that she had no desire for an impertinent phallus
that she only hallucinated her own angelic sex

---

*Lucian Blaga, major 20th-century modernist Romanian poet, one of the first influences on the poetry Andrei Codrescu wrote in his youth.

bleeding like a true underwater library
the books in her womb were the ornaments of souls reborn
which is why her hips flowered like a long-haired hawaiian goddess'
maybe the submarine was a lonely and shy phallus
maybe the submarine was a clumsy man unredeemed but clever
in any case the submarine began to rise skyward at a certain point
with the amerikan lying inside unshaven and partly in love
in wavy levitation like a cloudy earring
or maybe this was a truly sad situation
because the amerikan had a meteorite-hole within
and would have toyed with anything inflatable dolls and little motors
and loud parrots and the holy ghost and tarts in polka-dots and squares
with such hungry and restrained melancholy there is no surfacing
so when the amerikan took his one wing and rose skyward
the submarine followed erratically with the pianist right on it
rattling her hard she of the angel sex from the tarot
the submarine didn't rise like a helicopter or a harrier jet
but bolted haltingly a magical horse pouring odd objects from his ears
and after a spasm and a near-fall
after being a bit squished against the borders of the schizoidian ocean's
chasm
the phallic-headed submarine started straight up like an electric saw-fish
and cut through horizons and london fogs and the foam of baptism
like a funeral-dish fished out of a blessed corpse from whom the soul fled.
&
ah submarine evading all explanation
how beautiful you snaked away from interpreters
how well you resisted translation
how pleased we are that you allowed no psychoanalysis
with what sinuously drunk dance you eluded the flashlights
how quickly you changed your colors
how slick you became when you were caught

and how forcefully you shot out of the hands grabbing you
and how loyal you are to your mistress your maker
who named you muse even though you're cylindrical
you believe her unreservedly that you will arrive in the sky
even though you're an iron tear covered in waves of skin
you follow her like a puppy even though you're huge
and can move only when submerged
you watch over her sleep and drape yourself like an eyelid over her
when some amerikan tries to wake her up
how gorgeously you defend yourself from prose
how admirable your readiness to always believe
she imprinted you with belief from the first day when you were only sound
how well you feel without the weight of a brain or a heart
she thinks your thoughts and feels your feelings
you're happy like a lamb even if you're a skin-covered steel egg
you know that you're covered with worn words
you don't even want to read because she reads them out loud to you
and now and then turns them into music and plays
you adore music even if it's made from strident notes and filthy words
what a champ you are sub
look how she drags you after her toward the shore like a sparkling dress
and how little you care that the amerikan sees right through your bones
you're built randomly from splinters and dreams and a childishly drawn sex
caressed in your awkwardness called from the start angel and womb
my angel my womb hideout for the hidden angel angel in the womb
thus you were enchanted by the pianist even as she mended your rags
and wrapped you in steel bands oh you're a spoiled barrel you enchant me
you're a whim and a caprice but I don't admire your shape.

This excerpt from a collaborative book-length epic was written in Romanian by email by the two poets, published in a limited deluxe edition by Editura Brumar in Romania in 2007, and will appear in English in Codrescu's translation from Black Widow Press in 2009. In Romania, the Brumar book won the prize for the Best Poetry Book of 2007 from Radio-Arts Cultural. This fragment of the 70-page poem is the first publication in the U.S.

FOUR POEMS FROM *DAS AUGE DES ENTDECKERS*

by Nicolas Born
translated from German by Eric Torgersen

LANDSCAPE WITH BIG CAR

With such a big car we're bound to come through
dead or alive
in the back of the neck a music
that never stops
sweet air of Montana bitter air of Missouri
our coats billow out like we're on the run
we fill up
there are dog catchers running around loose
us in the sidelong looks of cowboys
us in the spendthrift shade of an airplane
us outside Chicago's field of fire
we shake hands with William Fulbright
we haunt our way through Arkansas
we visit a poet's grave in his lifetime
green all around with just a touch of yellow
the demonstration runs into the flames of Phoenix
Arizona redbrown outer space black
we're a point moving westwards
we're not Americans
but we're part of it too
a sheriff pulls us over
no we didn't pick up a black hitchhiker
we're not horse thieves but we are Germans
our politeness is the politeness of foreigners
we're getting faster
we feel like we're roaring
packed in sweet air
and in a music that never stops
we're aging really slowly
thank you Pentagon
for this statistical delaying effect

BEFORE FALLING ASLEEP

Under the covers three a.m.
I want to be off to the BETTER WORLD
this is the wall
I have to go into
to close off my face
and put the world behind me
in my own
personal past
The curtain's blowing it's September—
how silly these facts are
like the speech-spit
in the room
that drips
into my memory

"according to reliable sources"*
I'm already far away from myself
but I still feel me lying here
the one hand
mine
longingly around my balls
the other
mine
at my ear
the insertion point
into me
Here I am
voice
bones in the wall
I am you and sleeping

PARTING FOR LIFE AND PARTING FOR DEATH

How dead serious this coming and going
up ladders stairways
when someone turns away and actually
leaves with just a word
how empty the street is then
how left the one left is
how breathless and scared I follow
the flight and the chase over rooftops
beyond all feeling
and how I admire from a distance people
who part with a joke
and hug each other, terrified
yet then goodbye is just a hand
a tear on the platform
a spot of oil in the parking lot
and there really are people who go on living
somewhere else
and people of no return
goodbyes like rumpled beds and goodbyes like forgotten
toothbrushes
goodbyes out into the air
goodbyes for travel
and your soft goodbye to me
and my hoarse goodbye to you.
But a wave from the train station
is neither soft nor hoarse
and hearty handshakes mean
longer travels.
Everything behind your eyes is foreign to me
because you're a Colombian (but that's not the reason).
I give my father this hand
no one wants to tell him any more

*This is about the voice of a news announcer that makes it hard to sleep, which was supposed to be clearer at first, and also about the observation that we're glad to turn away from the world and toward the wall when going to sleep, while when waking we like to have the wall covering our backs and life in front of us, to get a view of it all. [Born's note, part of the poem—ET]

he's the spitting image of me
(I'm telling him here)
you hear me father!
where are your strong arms
have they grown far away from you
or have you just forgotten them in all
the resumes you had to write?
Goodbye!
And goodbye Uncle Heinrich
brother of my father
who was always just getting right up
from his crowded brown desk
goodbye old willow out my window in 1960
about which I made my first poem
because it brushed wearily on the windowpane
and always reminded me of something . . .
Here I get dizzy
because I'm almost alone already
with this pencil that's gone crazy
I stole it at Luchterhands
to get back at Roehler
who said my poem was larmoyant.
Poor dear Roehler
you can't even be larmoyant
goodbye then until the next pencil
and goodbye to Piwitt in Rome
who's burying the wrung dry
geniuses of sacred painting
one more time
and Buch who is one of the few you can
lend money to and to whom
being overweight is no big deal
goodbye Mother in the years after the war
who with her good hands switched pricetags
goodbye Günter Grass who works like a dog
but otherwise doesn't really do much
(maybe he has to because we all want it that way)
goodbye first wife
good morning second wife
goodbye old poet in me
always making pronouncements like
ONLY SOCIALISM WILL BRING
INDIVIDUALITY
which would be kind of late for my legs
which can't break out of this trot
goodbye Anna Karin Marianne Gisela
Barbara Margret Peter
goodbyes are still dead serious
and it's still not certain that goodbyes
are needed at all
it would be nicer to just go away
and just come back
and I would be happy if
when seen again this poem
from the middle on maybe
would be a little bit cheerful
which in fact it even is.

ON THE INSIDE OF POEMS

You can't make a living
competing with reality
you can't live on reality either
you can survive an operation
and get everything back
and go on through Life
through quickly fading pictures
that was you
you and the One in the Oven
Persons panting under their tombstones—
With unspeakable exertion
by you and all your ancestors
you shield yourself
Land and water remain
the sky remains
and you remain
you have nothing to get ready for
little suns light your democracy And
you choose life and death
you have many Beautiful Voices
you are many
your skin is your skin And finally
nothing but skin
you're the entrepreneur of Life
impresario of white apparitions
you're the Spaceman out in the universe
the author of the course of history
you can print time like books
you dice and sieve and love And the ruins
of dictating machines are blowing in the wind
unreason is in full bloom
you're the bloom and the unreason
you're day and night in the day and at night
you're the killer
circling through your own veins
you're father and son
you're the slaughtered Indian
and the registered Indian
you're all colors and races
you're the widows and orphans
you're the prisoners' uprising
you're a howling that never ends
knife-throws shots
you're the fantastic athlete of the Dream Miles
the iconoclast in the head of democracy
you're the master chain-breaker
you're the secretly shining phrase
the pennant
the avant garde of the Free Kitchens
you're Man And
Beast when it senses death
you're alone and you're everyone
you're your death and you're the Great Wish
you're the map you're spreading out And
you're your death

BEAUTIFUL BY NIGHT

by Noam Mor

Where is my desire? In the way he walks.

An absence that drives me to someone else's breath. The way in which a human being ripens. My unfulfilled boiling to some sense of fruitlessness. A thing who desires things he cannot know. Husband and Wife walk about each other, know each's place in their crossings.

He tells me, I walked to my Azzahra. Recounts following them. I follow those who walk to the ones they desire. Repeat him though I'm not even witness, my soul's reduction. My feet falter like drizzle. A pretence without legs. Flotsam and words. I would take him deep in my lungs. Always in a state of hunger.
Will I never know their names?
If only I. Strangers, we fall behind them, waiting till they are lost.

He continues, Humdulillah, God Is Great, for they had come to me on such a day, my pockets empty. The wind tosses a bedsheet across the rooftops above our heads. Approaching her husband, she brushes his hand. They didn't ask the way. Faltering headfirst without knowing. Fools. Both Husband and I looked at his wife to be sure she was safe. There is nothing but waiting. Humdulillah, God is great, for they had only to walk on.

1

Blasphemy upon our fathers! Though his story will end and my hunger remain, I reach for him from a great distance. A single measure on the landscape, I try to leave two sets of footprints, be two clots of land, though I am not my storyteller's legs or roots. I have no grip. No satisfaction in the knowledge I call mine, my coffee-stained gallabiya a shade of no consequence. The winter billows the long dress of my gallabiya and I begin counting. Counting calms me. I open my eyes.

He tells me, I waited. Her back was a map of my Azzahra's spine, from her thick shoulders to her wide hips, wife that once filled my hands. Locked in her eyes as they were joyful for me, gamillah de'lilah, beautiful by night.

I hid in the crowd as she looked back.

Insha'allah, the will of Allah, Still remembering. I moved to the City of the Dead after casting her out. Mourned for though she isn't even dead. Her small hands had lain over me, black cat's paws kneading. Could I have remained with her? Husband and Wife haven't seen me. When can they know they are lost?

I continue, Husband faces an alley blankly. Wife raises her palms upward, elbows bent.

Do you know where we are? This isn't on the map.
A boy jokes with him, asks if he wants a shoeshine though he wears sandals, but he doesn't understand. The boy laughs.

Marhab huwagga, Welcome stupid foreigner.
Without a decision between them, Husband points at a minaret and crescent.

We should move on.

He then tells a girl who has begged he has no pen though he has one in his pocket. He slackens his pace to be beside Wife. She lets his arm take her. Just come with me, he tells her.

Keep walking keep walking, we whisper.

He watches the cinderblock buildings. The terraces bend over them as Wife walks in tight steps just ahead, her hands kept in her pockets and her shoulders hunched. A tide of people open before him and close around her, pilings thickening the space between them. Wrapping my kafiya tightly around my head, my gallabiya pulled against me, I join them, watch her large hips, her exposed hair, a shiver in the current.

He continues, I had not kept my Azzahra. I wanted to meet her eyes as she looked at him. Husband reminds me of a woman walking behind his woman, a drop of seed behind her. He looks back many times. As if he might touch her. Men on scooters honk beside them, thick like sand, pressing them further into the street. She looks behind herself many times. Both stare at a woman passing. Her entire body hidden, sunglasses over her eyes and her hands in white gloves. Women begin to wail before a house nearby, wagging their tongues at high pitch. For Azzahra, my juliet, at her exile, many women keened, a swarm of indistinct bodies and heads covered in gallabiyas and higabs, casting me the evil eye. Locusts. Insha'allah, my luck changed that day.

The couple is drawn to the dirge. The women's howls grow as they thicken at the door.
Had they understood the sorrow?
Her husband steps onto the balcony, complains that his children weep.

My son wishes that you bless his mother into God's ears, not like dogs. Stop and get to your homes! Go to her grave in three days. Do not cry here!

I too had told them stop howling like dogs before Allah, who says all that rises from the hand and the mouth is evil. Stop this blasphemy and accept my wife's exile. Go to Azzahra's family tomb. Do not remind me. What I had done. I have sat in my darkened living room, smoking cigarette after cigarette too nauseated to eat, wondering, insha'allah, when will this be forgotten? I have dreamt of women, heads covered in silk higabs of purple, red, ochre and orange, embroidered with stars like mosque tiles.
Beautiful birds moving across the city, they are plentiful, an irresistible landscape of women. Azzahra breaks off from the flock and enters a villa, her gallabiya Cleopatra purple with pink sides. I become Yusuf in a jacket of gold thread, vines circling roses, my head surrounded in flame. In the first room, Azzahra reaches out to me, a temptress leading me through seven more, waiting for seduction, but I do not stir. She had embraced another man and though she is beautiful and the paintings of our consummation stir me, refresh me, I can no longer fulfill her. She locks the door of each room until we are in the seventh. Humdulilah, God is great, just as Allah helped Yusuf thrust off the temptress Zulayka, God opens the door for me so I can escape Azzahra's temptation. I sway at the abyss beyond the doors. I feel her arms around me in our last days as Azzahara and I no longer knew I cared for her.

I go on, Wife turns toward us. I become a scabbed dog, reach for her, much of my hind legs scratched clear of hair. She pulls back, holds her husband's arm. I imagine the warmth of his body, my paleness envious of his solidity. I am hobbled by how to be. What I am not. I must catch her eyes as she looks at him. The minarets dominate three compass directions like buoys against the sky, a landscape of squat earth-brown homes around us. A young boy sits on a low bench beside a table before a dull blue wall. The boy smiles widely when Wife walks to him.

Marhaba.

He waves his hand over wood carvings of geometrical designs.

Abuya hamel'hum.

He picks one and hands it to her. As she looks, his father pays for his coffee and hurries over.

Marhaba.

The woodcarver asks her how much she will pay. Everyone waits. Husband looks into the square. Wife asks him how much he wants, handing it to him, but he does not open his hand, asks her to start with a price so they can negotiate. She offers a small part of where he wishes to begin and he smiles politely.

Offer me a fair price and I will give you the carving, just for the wood and a small amount for my work.

He puts his hand to his chest and she listens carefully, understands a little for she offers a slightly higher price for the carving and puts it on the table. Husband rocks as she bargains. The son wants to help his father, so picks up different carvings and tilts them toward her.

My father made these.
She smiles at him and he looks away, scraping his foot over the ground, smiling for her. She looks at a mosque design of one six-pointed star within another, enclosed in a twelve-sided figure, one leading into another, producing an infinite series of the same until it spills outside the square. Husband gestures to her, then the street and carvings, touches his pants gently like his skin, purses his lips. She puts her hand out, palm open and waits.

The woodcarver's son runs to make change. He offers them some tea, but they will not have any, do not wish to understand the custom of a sale. The woodcarver points to the cafe opposite, at the carving she holds. They shake their heads but he still calls for three teas. He readjusts his kafiya round his head and neck in the light cast by the weakening sun. In these few minutes, Wife rubs her fingers across the table, quiet but for the sound of the wind flapping against two kites battling in the sky over the square.

Humdulillah.

The woodcarver raises his cup, sips. He loses interest in them, squats on a badly stained pillow and continues carving. Wife shivers and I feel cold in the lull. They do not try to speak with each other.

The woodcarver hums. Husband taps his fingers on his table. We both sit at the cafe and wait for Husband and Wife to walk on. Exhaling into a sheesha bowl, we listen to water mumbling, the time passing with our breath. Under our eyelids sunlight pulses like a veil.

He reflects, A man I may never find. Insha'allah, I had witnessed Azzahra's lips waiting for him, a hidden kiss under the arch of the doorway, the tilt of her head, imagined the touch of his lips. Other witnesses and the story spread. A deep stain on our houses, the tombs of our forebears, impoverished end in shame. I did not know I was happy until I had cast her out and I want her though she kissed another when some time may pass. But how?

I had come to Cairo from fields of cotton in the delta near Beni Suef, rows of flowering bushes with pale yellow organs, petals collapsing into flecks of white for the harvest. A fertile soil of what is not mine but my brothers' and their families. Too many for the soil, left to struggle by with my portion of harvest pulled from this city. So much of this country dust that there is no place within it that allows me to wish. I am the dust.

Wife recognizes us. I fly with the little boy's kite to escape. Husband and Wife watch me bob in the wind. Be careful of the strong wind, the young girl says to her brother, rubbing her string against his. South, the silver domes and two sharp and high minarets of the Muhammad Ali Mosque cast a shadow on the hill behind it. Minarets float over the apartment complexes like bee hives as far as the horizon, the roofs covered in rubble or wash or bare, some with makeshift shelters of sheets and blinds. My string snaps and I am spiralling in the muzzy sky, cut loose. I hit the ground, am absorbed by it only to be spit back, to look at her, her eyes bordered by a wide line of charcoal and her thick black hair loose.

It is our poverty to smoke sheesha alone.

2

The woodcarver's boy yells as the sun falls low. They look for us but we have moved. I brush close to her, my Khafiya wrapped against her recognition. Cornering her blue eyes.

Muttering, Shokran, Thank you. Wife looks aside. Husband should keep a better eye on the woman of his family.

He asks, Had I?

Husband glances back often for his wife, yet hasn't noticed me. Busy looking at so much he saw so little. She wanders to a vegetable cart, denuded prickly pears and carrots on either side of red chili peppers piled thick in a pyramid. She brushes her cheeks with the trunks of a prickly pear's thorns until her face is red. Husband turns against the tide of people, pushing against them. He leans beside her ear, touching her shoulder. Habbibi, I imagine him saying, speaking into her ear.

Had Azzahra kissed him? I called her name many times in the street, hoping she would respond. Azzahra had wished to know my wishes, insha'allah, for a short while, but in my anger I no longer told her.
Wife places her arm through his and chides him, comfort in the chiding.

As Azzahra would. It would be so had I known the way.
Holding her arm, he focusses skyward, up at the laundry hanging from crumbling cement balconies, windows without glass but cloth, and gate lattices made of rebar. The dust of brown sand has settled on the paved roadways and cinderblock buildings. He points at a carved screen of a five-pointed star, its design lost in a history of dryness and wind and attempts at repair with little money or skill. He enjoys this deteriorating mashrabiyyah. I cannot find his pleasure in the worn carvings. He cannot provide direction, whispers and releases her arm. Offers her no strength. Lay? Why?

God be with them. A woman must support her husband even when he is a fool. A woman stands before her tent of filthy rugs, a bedouin before her cooking fire, covered in a black burkha, metal trinkets dangling like silver coins below her eyes and bosom. Barefoot, her toes are spread wide before a pile of bricks in the open lot amongst the roofless remains of a building. Around the remains of a fountain, her goats and donkey eat. She shakes her trinkets at Husband and Wife, her walls reduced to rubbish in a patch of bright winter sun.

Marhab!

Both finally sure they are lost. Wife looks for the street on their map, at most an ummarked white line. I come beside her and take the map from her small hands, brushing her, May I help you? They do not answer, look to one another, Husband drawing closer to his wife, May I draw a line on your map where you go? I ask Wife. After a moment of silence, I point.

This is where you stand.

Have you followed us? Husband asks.

I am a guide. My job is to follow the people and lead them the right way. I must know where you are going.

Metro, she says. I point west, to the Sultan Mu'ayyad Mosque, Turn left at that mosque and you will be near your destination. I gesture with a scalloped slice of my hand and a jerk of my head, but Husband shakes his head without understanding. I ask him for some money and he offers me little. Thanking him, I ask for more, but he refuses, La basheesh. Basheesh la. He waves his hands and head in a clear no, as if I do not understand Arabic, Ya'la! Ya'la! Go! Go! He tries to brush me away. I stop and wave my hand before my face like a slap, wish to smack him, but she says, Ana asif, I am sorry. And I thank her, Let me take you to the Blue Mosque. Come this way. We are near.

I do not tell him there is no Metro at Aqsunqur. Insha'allah, It was his decision not to increase the basheesh and the rest follows. A man like him should become lost and so shall she, the way of things.

I Leave them and they go on without me.

3

It will do them good to become lost. I run. Am surprised I run. I breathe and it tastes like him. I had survived on his residue, what was heard. For as long as I resloved to be him, he sheltered me. I was fed. I sit in the archway of a building, the roof lined with mullions shaped like a row of pointed arrowheads, roll a cigarette and huddle to keep warm. Husband looks up at the evening, worries about the namelessness of the sky. I watch the narrow confines that surround them as his wife walks just paces behind him. I must look into her eyes as she looks at him.

Come, he presses Husband and Wife on, You will know where you are soon.

He wishes to go to the Blue Mosque to look for his Azzahra. Husband waits for his wife to reach him and they begin walking side by side, but still does not take her arm. They whisper so I cannot hear them and continue their ambivalent walk. The muezin's call to prayer breaks over the streets. They listen to the singing of his name, still finding it wondrous. It hardly awakens me. Husband looks but does not recognize me. A group of children play a game of soccer around them kicking a flattened water jug. Wife stands still at a painted wedding announcement, hugs herself against the cooling sky. A bride in western gown, a triangle of face mostly dark eyes and mouth, her groom in black gallabiyah embroidered in gold thread. They stand in a rich oasis of bright yellow and orange sand, a pool of blue water fills the painting to the horizon. The rest of the house collapsed stones. Husband touches her shoulder as she wraps her scarf more tightly. She leans toward him to ask for him. Again to her she brings his hand. He caresses her soft cheeks.

This way, this way to your destination.

What are your names? I am not heard.

Husband slows to be with her, walks beside her and she slips her arm through his, invites him to hold her, the sky just before darkness. Wife stops and smells perfume; jasmine, hibiscus, rose and sandalwood, musk and rosewood in small glass bottles. She passes the perfume to her husband, thick with scent. The perfumer hands her a bottle, looks between them and laughs. She puts two drops of jasmine round her neck, gently chides her husband again for comfort. He must smell the scent, Azzahra's favorite scent. At the Blue Mosque, they find no Metro. They struggle to see the pattern of five-pointed stars covering the dome, the gold crescents of the minarets in the darkness. Husband's voice rises, his hands small in the place they take in.

4

Are we still lost?

From this distance, they can see tombs, domed and brown like the earth, scattered minarets, simple sarcophagi of stone dotting the blurry landscape. Wife points at children playing in the cemetery and a woman walking across it, not a visitor, but entering a tomb. A cab passes and they take it.

I look over The City of the Dead. In the northwest corner, obscured by the distance and the settling darkness is his Azzahra, dung-brown and thick rope-like strands of stone forming her dome. She must be home, for it is night. Gamillah de'lilah. Beautiful under moonlight. My facts fall like rain. I reach to play with the warmth of bodies. None close nor kin. I lean over the wall, retch. Faith in me scarce. Hold me. Me. Me.

PLUNGE POOL

by Garry Craig Powell

Marwan was in a boutique in the Burjuman Center, buying lingerie for his Syrian secretary, when he felt the heat of a stare on him. He spun round and there, to his terror, was Randa, looking like an Egyptian queen, peering in through the window with one eyebrow raised and her upper lip lifting in a sneer. He was clutching a black lace babydoll—caught red-handed. Then he remembered: Randa wasn't his wife any more. She had no right to judge him. He could march out and indignantly put her in her place, or keep flirting with the Algerian salesgirl.

Before he could do either, Randa spoke to a big bearded man in Gulf dress who stood beside her. She nodded at Marwan, twisting her lips as if she were sucking a lemon. How could she stoop so low? A local! Marwan hadn't missed her since the divorce, but all of a sudden he needed her violently. For now, though, he could do nothing but complete his purchase.

The salesgirl, who was alluring in a bulging blouse and thin pants, had her crimson lips puckered in astonishment, or ridicule. She must have understood the dumb show.

"I'll take it," Marwan said, cursing his luck. He could hardly ask her for a date now.

He called Randa's cell phone but she didn't answer. He left messages. That night he took Ghada, the secretary, to Lord Jim's, where she coaxed him into swaying under the matting and masks and dugout canoes, to the rhythms of a Cuban band. Back in his apartment he asked her to model the babydoll. Ghada looked luscious as she bent over in the bathroom, and yet she was too compliant for his taste. If only she'd put up a fight. Randa had always teased, made him feel that he had to take her by force, which was tantalizing and exciting.

"*Shu hada, habibi?*" Ghada asked when he stopped touching her. *What's up, darling?*

"I'm just not in the mood," he snapped in Arabic. "Get dressed and make some tea."

Ghada blanched, pulled her panties on, murmured "Yes, sir," and went to the kitchen. Bare but for an undershirt and black socks, Marwan lit a cigarette on the edge of the bathtub. The pink marble and gold fittings made him feel a fraud. It was like the nightmare where he turned up for an examination, naked from the waist down, his penis drooping like the tail of a scared dog. What had he done? Why had it taken him until now to see that he needed his wife? And why did he need her? Sucking on the cigarette, momentarily soothed, he looked in the mirror and saw Saad, his murdered brother. *You need the bitch because she makes you feel like me. Like a man.* Yes, that was it. If he was honest with himself, he didn't love her, never had, and yet he couldn't live without her either. As soon as he could get rid of Ghada, he'd call Randa again.

He ordered a Ghazal taxi; the Mercedes would soften Ghada's resentment. After she'd gone, in tears, he poured a scotch and gazed out of the window at the illuminated glass towers and the rivers of red and white lights far below. His life was as sterile as Dubai. At thirty-four, he was childless. Why had he married the barren slut? Because she too was a Palestinian refugee and he'd been homesick in the States. Why didn't she love him? Truly, he was an unlucky man. He hadn't seen Randa for two months, had no idea where she lived. He wrote her an e-mail and typed *Fayruz* as the subject. Randa would open that for sure. If he claimed that his sister had urged him to reconcile with his ex-wife, was that so immoral? The ends justified the means.

He sent Randa a heart-rending plea. He couldn't live without her. He had been wrong to divorce her. She was right, his fault had been as great as hers. He should never have been on LebaneseLovers.com. And when Randa had walked into the café for her date—when he discovered that it was Randa he'd been flirting with all along—he should have had a sense of humor. He didn't mention his shame and anger, or bring up the Emirati gorilla. Before he went to bed, he spent an hour poring over pictures of Brazilian underwear models, but manfully restrained himself from masturbating. He'd save up his lust for Randa.

With a fawning smile, the Filipina gestured toward a bench covered with a white sheet. Candles burned in the windowless room. It was a cave, filled with unsettling aromas. Marwan saw himself through the girl's eyes: without his suit he was a puny figure in flip-flops and undershirt, a striped towel wrapped around his waist; a curly, clean-shaven, expat Arab. A nobody. Was this how Randa saw him? His sense of self flickered and threatened to gutter.

"Sir, there's anything you need?" Was she inviting him to make a pass? In Dubai you never knew. The Filipina looked as ingenuous as a schoolgirl. What if he pushed her onto the bench? Would she dare resist? But no, this was a high-class hotel, nothing like the sleazy place by the Fish Roundabout with the Chinese masseuse who wore stockings and heels. Besides, he'd be seeing Randa soon. He could scarcely believe that she'd consented to meet him. For now, he had to relax. Relax, relax. Be like Saad. "I'm fine," he said, pulling himself together.

"Mr. Tyrone will be with you presently, sir," the girl said, withdrawing.

He lay down and shut his eyes. The room was silent, an anchorite's cell. God, if the old bastard existed, could hear his shameful thoughts. Only when Marwan heard a click, then rushing water, wind, and songbirds, was he aware that someone had entered and switched on a stereo. He opened his eyes. A man in a short-sleeved white smock loomed over him.

"Good afternoon, sir. I am Tyrone."

He was a powerful-looking Sri Lankan of forty-five or so with receding black hair and a handsome face that had the color and luster of coffee beans. Marwan had ridiculed his western friends' gushing reverence for the masseur, and yet, to his surprise, his first impression was of a man who was serene and wise, a sage. In spite of himself, he trusted him at once.

Tyrone didn't look directly at Marwan. "You don't mind the tape, sir?"

Marwan rolled his head from side to side. The waterfall on the soundtrack sluiced through the top of his head, cleansed his lungs of fog or smoke, and golden light poured into his chest. Tyrone hadn't even touched him yet. Marwan's body was filling with helium, floating upward. Was it autosuggestion? It couldn't be joy, surely?

"Shall I take my shirt off?" he asked.

Tyrone nodded. No fussing.

"My boxers?"

"Not necessary, sir."

Relieved, Marwan sat up and removed his shirt. Saad had probably never given his manhood a thought until the Christians had cut his throat during the Sabra massacre in 1982. What would *he* have done with the Chinese masseuse? *I'd have given her one.* She'd kept pressing those hard little oranges into Marwan's back, and rolled down his shorts, squeezed his buttocks; but he'd been more embarrassed than excited. In spite of her fishnet stockings and spikes, Marwan hadn't been sure if sex was on offer, and hadn't dared ask.

Tyrone was unstopping glass phials and mixing oils. What, God forbid, if Marwan got hard? He reclined on his elbows, trying to look casual, proud of the black fur on his chest. Randa always said that Arabs were the only real men, a sentiment echoed by his sister. Then why had Fayruz married a lily-white Englishman? And why had Randa married him? He was a Levantine, a city boy, a softie, not Bedu, not a true Arab.

"Could you lie on your stomach, sir?"

With his arms stiff against his sides

and his neck twisted, one cheek on the sheet, Marwan felt like a tourist on Jumeirah Beach. Tyrone anointed his feeble arms, gently pinching his flesh, pressing his palms, pulling his fingers. The Sri Lankan turned his attention to his back, pouring on oil, rubbing it into his dry skin, poking and prodding at the knots in his neck and shoulders.

"I didn't realize I was so tense," Marwan said. "Those muscles are pretty bad, eh?"

"So-so, sir. Some of my clients are worse." His voice was as soft and soothing as Pan Pipes. "There is so much stress in people's lives nowadays."

"I'm stuck in a traffic jam for an hour every morning."

"May I ask where you work, sir?" Tyrone was working on Marwan's shoulders, pushing down, rubbing them, teasing the tangled fibers. It hurt.

"I'm an investment advisor in a bank," Marwan mumbled, mouth open like a fish's.

With his fingertips, Tyrone played quiet chords all over Marwan's back. "I'm sorry, sir."

Sorry? Had he misunderstood? If not, was he being rude or sympathetic? What was wrong with being a banker? The waterfall cascaded, tropical birds hooted and cried, Marwan smelled sandalwood and cedar. "And I got divorced a couple of months ago," he blurted out.

Tyrone put the heels of his palms on Marwan's back and pushed down on him as if he were half-drowned. "Excellent," Tyrone said. Marwan was about to ask what the hell he meant when his breath was knocked out of him. A thunderstorm of blows swept over his back.

"Where did you learn all this?" Marwan gasped.

"Mostly from my uncle, sir, but I've taken courses in Sweden and Thailand too."

"Really? You strike me as a man made for higher things. You could be a manager."

"A few months ago I was promoted to Front Desk Manager, sir."

"What happened?"

"Well sir, three Emirati boys attacked a prostitute in one of our rooms while I was on duty, and she asked me to call the police. They demoted me, sir. I was lucky to keep my old job."

Marwan's mouth was squashed into the sheet. It smelled of mothballs. "A man of integrity," he muttered.

Tyrone covered Marwan's back with the towel and oiled his thighs and calves, kneading them, pummeling them with karate chops. Marwan had always thought of his body as a possession, like his car, which he would have upgraded if he could. Now he understood that he *was* his body. Wasn't this why he had married Randa, because she had given him the gift of his body, made him feel it, nailed it to his brain?

"I wish I had your courage," he said, as Tyrone pressed his thumbs into the soles of his feet. What was possessing him? He sounded like a schoolboy with a crush.

Tyrone was rotating Marwan's feet, wiggling and pulling his toes.

"So what should I do, Tyrone?"

"Would you turn on to your back, sir?"

Marwan took care to hold onto the towel. With his chest exposed he felt vulnerable. But the masseur's eyes were as deep and placid as a deer's.

Tyrone poured oil onto Marwan's chest. It was disquieting to have a man pressing down on his breast. Marwan's arms were stiff as broomsticks. His voice came out strangled. "I feel bad about the divorce. I'm thinking of getting back with my wife. Do you think I should?"

An electric current pulsed through his penis. It tingled, not pleasurably, thank God, but like when, after a long ride on his racing bike in his student days in Albany, he'd dismounted.

"I don't know, sir," said Tyrone. There was nothing erotic in the way he rubbed his chest.

"Don't be so noncommittal. Come on, out with it." It was the tone he used with Ghada. A crease appeared in Tyrone's forehead. He uncovered Marwan's legs but didn't reply.

"I didn't mean to speak like that,"

Marwan said.

"It isn't my place to tell you what to do, sir. No one can do that for anyone else."

"But what would you do? You're a Buddhist, aren't you? What does your religion say?"

Tyrone rubbed Marwan's knees. "According to the Dhammapada, we must practice right speech, right thoughts, and right action."

Marwan couldn't help groaning as Tyrone oiled and squeezed his thighs. "The Prophet Mohammed, peace be upon him, says the same." Tyrone's strong fingers slid up towards Marwan's groin. He was getting bigger, surely just because it was warmer all of a sudden. It wasn't a hard-on, it was just a little turgid. A tremor ran through his body; tears pricked his eyes. The water and wind and birds had fallen silent; weird flutes and drums took their place. How had it got so hot? Sweat trickled from his armpits, down his chest and thighs. Tyrone stared, unblinking, like Saad, his father, like God. Marwan burst out: "I divorced her, it's true, but she was planning to meet another man. She was on an online dating site. Imagine! I know because I was the man she met. Can you believe that we arranged to meet each other? Was that fate? She said I should forgive her because I was equally to blame. But I'm a man, I can't help myself. I'm screwing my secretary. Is that wrong? It is, isn't it? Do you despise me?"

Tyrone's voice mingled with the flutes and drums. "Please calm yourself, sir. I despise nobody. Is it wrong for you to sleep with your secretary? If she has surrendered to you because she's afraid, then it is bad. Does she love you? Do you love her? Only you can answer these questions." The heat throbbed; the A/C must have broken down. The oils were overpowering.

Marwan pictured Randa, sullen and naked, in the white, gilt-edged bed, under the chandelier. Randa grappling with him, cantankerous, elusive. The flutes warbled; the drums pounded like a migraine. He'd wanted to love her. He'd tried. She reeked of French scent, sweat and cigarettes. When she was depressed she didn't shower—which was oddly arousing.

"I love you," he said. "I mean *her*, of course."

"Of course, sir."

Marwan babbled: "I'm grateful for your advice, Tyrone, and for your example too. I admire you. I like you—I don't *love* you, haha. I'm going to do the right thing. *Insha'allah*. I will ask my ex-wife to come back. You see what an effect you've had on me?"

Tyrone pulled the towel up to Marwan's chest—and Marwan saw his erection. As if he'd noticed nothing, Tyrone dimmed the lights and tiptoed out, leaving Marwan in the hot cave, with the shrilling flutes, the hammering drums, the smell of sandalwood and cedar, and his shame.

He was to meet Randa now, at four, and could have waited for her, but he felt self-conscious loitering outside the sauna. Besides, through the window he could see a woman in a black one-piece bathing suit, who was striking even in the dim amber glow. He blundered in and gasped. In a steam bath you could at least breathe, but the Swedes had devised a torture that sucked the air out of your lungs, singed your skin, and made your heart race.

"*Salaam alaiykum*," he said breathlessly.

"*Walaiykum a salaam*."

A Gulf accent, although she had short-cropped hair and bare limbs, which she didn't try to conceal with her towel. Dubai girls were notorious, but still Marwan was amazed to find an Arab woman in the mixed sauna. She sat on the top pine bench and eyed him shamelessly. He lay down on the lowest of the slatted benches, wishing he cut a more prepossessing figure. He inhaled the scent of eucalyptus. His skin burned. He wouldn't be able to stand it for long.

Randa's arrival struck him like a punch. She was wearing a scandalous bikini, although Marwan had to admit she still had the figure for it. With a dipper she poured water onto the iron grid; it sizzled like a barbecue. Steam bloomed, and for a moment he could breathe.

"Let's go somewhere else," he said in Arabic.

"I've just arrived." Randa settled on a top bench. To Marwan it was like having two panthers poised above him.

"How can we talk in this furnace?" he said, switching to English. "And what about her?"

"I don't give a shit," Randa said in the New York accent she'd picked up in Albany, where they'd met as students. Her face was incandescent. "Bet she doesn't understand, anyway."

She was going to call the shots, then. "So what do you think?" he said.

Randa shut her eyes, turned into a blind priestess. "I don't *think*."

"You must think something." He wanted to stroke her smooth, shiny legs.

She opened her eyes. They burned. "This is what you wanted, no?" she intoned.

"It was a mistake."

"I am content."

"With that Emirati?" he sneered. The other girl raised her eyebrows.

"He's good to me," Randa said. "I have a flat in Jumeirah Beach. A sporty Mazda."

"What are you saying? Aren't you ashamed to be that animal's mistress? Is that how you want to live, like a whore? Don't you think of me? My mother's visiting for Eid Al Fitr. She doesn't even know we're divorced yet. What am I going to tell her?"

The Emirati girl muttered something in Arabic to Randa.

"*Shu?*" Marwan said.

Fixing him with her sloe eyes, the girl with the close-cropped hair repeated the Arab proverb: *A man with no beard is like a garden without flowers.*

"How dare you interfere?" He meant to intimidate her the way he did with his inferiors at the bank, but his voice came out high and nasal, petulant. The heat was crushing him.

"Fuck you," the Emirati girl said in English. Randa gave a hissing sigh and wrapped her towel around herself. With her disheveled hair, she looked sultry, inviting, forbidding.

"Can we talk a little more?" Marwan said, following her into the chilly corridor.

"I'm going to the plunge pool."

He prayed no one he knew would see him, a man, following her. In the wet room, an elderly Arab sat in the Jacuzzi with a couple of giggling Filipina girls.

"Can't we try again?" Marwan asked her as they reached the edge of the pool.

"You should jump in now, while you're hot," she said.

"Randa, I need you," he pleaded. "I don't think I'm going in. It's freezing, isn't it?"

"It's refreshing. You feel great afterwards."

"You go first."

"No, you."

He unwound his towel and tossed it on a recliner. If he leapt in, she might be impressed.

"I'm not such a wimp as you think," he told her, but before he could brace himself, she shoved him. The water was icy, the pain startling. He flailed, scrabbled to the surface, spitting and sputtering, his heart stunned. As he threshed to the side of the pool, he gasped, but the cold and the shock were so intense that he couldn't draw breath. Panic seized him. Saad was standing beside Randa, scarred and mutilated and potent, even in death, bursting with murderous sexual energy. *These might be your last moments,* his brother told him, his words reverberating in the bare chamber. *How do you feel about that?*

If he ever drew breath again, if he lived, he'd cast off his fear and act like a man from now on. Always. He was sure. Marwan lunged at Randa's leg but it was sticky with sweat and his fingers slipped off. She was right by the edge and could have reached out to help him. But she looked down on him with the malice of a stone goddess. *Are you ready now?* Saad demanded in his eerie echoing voice. *Are you ready?*

Not yet, brother. Not yet, not yet, not yet.

FROM *THE EGYPTIAN CHRONICLES: A FULLBRIGHT MEMOIR*

by Dawn-Michelle Baude

A part of a hoof. Then an ear. I can't figure out why so many body parts are mixed with the rubbish.

"Mom, there's a horn."

"Maybe it's from the same animal."

We walk a little further down the street.

"No," Alex says. "Here's part of a leg. It's black—the ear was white." He prods it with his shoe.

I discourage direct examination of refuse.

"I'm not touching it!" He veers suddenly to the left, near an overflowing trashcan. "Look, Mom—a hoof! A perfect hoof!"

It lies there in a pile of fine gravel, its enamel gleaming in the sun.

We walk on, thoroughly fascinated by the trash at our feet. And besides, if we keep our eyes down, we can avoid meeting the stares from other pedestrians and completely ignore our surveillance in the slum towers that line the road.

"Why are there so many needles?"

"People are doing drugs—see? There's a bottle." I'm not sure methadone comes in a bottle like that, but the object has some sort of illicit quality about it, guilt by association with syringe.

I spot a tail next to a gummy cola can. "Looks like a sheep."

Alex stands over the amputated patch of fur. "Sheep," he concludes solemnly. "How come Egyptians leave sheep parts everywhere?"

"That's it!" Some neglected neural net surged to life. "You don't remember the sheep slaughtered on our front steps in Beirut."

He was too young, and I didn't let him watch. Blood stained our porch for days. It faded from brick to brown to grey, and finally wore away.

"Gross," frowns Alex. "Wow—there's a really good horn. Can I keep it?"

No.

"For the Aïd holiday," I recall. "It's sorta like Christmas, only Muslims eat lamb." The slaughtering follows very strict guidelines with lots of prayers and verses from the Qur'an. "The butcher knows exactly where to place the knife so that the sheep doesn't suffer—it's a lot like the kosher traditions of the Jews."

The similarities among Semitic peoples seem to outweigh their differences, once the weapons are taken away.

"In fact, hallal and kosher butchering is more humane than Western slaughterhouses where the animals are traumatized en masse and die a painful death."

"I don't want to talk about it."

Then Alex adds, "If the horn's still there when we get back, can I have it?"

*****

WESTERNER NEEDS TAXI.

As soon as my arm goes up—one swoops to the curb.

"Mumkin Carrefour Mall?"

The young man at the wheel, his dashboard lined with Nubian tassels, nods.

While the man in the passenger seat looks at us coolly, the woman sitting in the back scoots over. Her head is covered in a hijab, but her eyes are visible. They are bright and wide with surprise, shiny stars.

Alex hesitates. "Mom, there's a veiled person in the back seat."

"Taxis are shared here," I say in French as we squeeze in. "The drivers can't make enough money off one fare so they have to combine riders."

I'd learned this particular point of taxi etiquette in Lebanon where I had harangued a taxi driver from Hamra all the way to the Ecole des Beaux Arts, thinking he was taking advantage of me by loaning the taxi ride I'd paid for to other people.

Wrong. The other riders paid, too. Just like here.

Our fellow passengers look at us curiously as they come and go in the other seats, as if we are stray parts of the body politic, odd bits that have somehow ended up in a broken-down taxi wheezing its way through the most densely populated country in the Middle East where over one-third of the region's population lives and kids drink from sewers. But in the last ten years, Mubarak's policies and kick-backs have apparently created a middle class, enough of them to warrant a shopping mall on the outskirts of Alexandria—or maybe the mall survives on the Persian Gulf influx during the scorching summer months when Alexandria's population swells to the point of paralysis.

The mall seems incongruous in the dun-colored landscape, all glass and marble and neon. It's more like a movie set than a shopping center, a kind of surreal icon of the US suburbs displaced to the shores of the fetid Lake Maryut, the ancient waterway from Alexandria to the Nile now silted up and home to families living in squalor.

"Maybe there's a Chucky Cheese!" says a hopeful Alex, as we drive across the parking lot to the grand entrance that tries a little too hard to be impressive. The colorful signage and buoyant architecture seem somehow suspect, like a woman with too much perfume.

I hand the driver 15 Egyptian pounds through the open car window. It's important to pay when you're out of the car so that if an altercation with the driver ensues, you can steel yourself and walk away.

"I'm sorry, but the fare is twenty dollars," the driver says in perfect English. He might speak French, too. He's been listening to us talk the whole way. He probably has a graduate degree in engineering or political science. He's lucky. He has a job.

"La'," I reply. "Khamastãshar."

"Twenty," he insists. The driver is doing this, I'm certain, because we're foreign.

"Khamastashar da sah." Fifteen is right, I protest, though I wonder, for a second, if Fatima has told me the wrong price. "Ana sekna hena." I live here.

"Iskandria?" The driver is befuddled.

I nod.

"OK." He raises the money to his lips and kisses it tenderly, intimately, the way a lover presses his lips on the hand of his beloved.

Alex plows through the sliding-glass doors of the entryway, confident in known circumstances.

I follow.

*****

And just like that, the nature of reality changes. The film between worlds is thinner than we often think, more like the skin of a bubble than the heavy velvet weight of the curtains on stage.

Inside the mall, everything is bright and shiny and new, muzak in the background, potted ferns thriving in the atrium light, the fronds reaching toward the skylight with tiny, determined fingers. Many women are showing their hair—some are even dressed like westerners, in tight jeans and transparent shirts—they must have come here in chauffeur-driven Mercs. They are probably educated Coptic Christians or Muslims from liberal families. I unbutton my black coat and drape it over my arm, slide my hat into my backpack while Alex makes a beeline to the entertainment center, his kid radar honed by previous challenges. After the bumper cars, bungee ropes, moonwalks and slides, we find a Western-style café.

It isn't exactly Marilyn's Pie Shop in downtown Belleville, Illinois, but some fiber of recognition seems to beckon from the refrigerated vat ringed by strands of attractive plastic ivy where the tuna salad is heaped in decorative mounds like a landmark of youth, some mini-Mount Rushmore of the protein and fat variety. You can take the girl out of the Midwest, but you can't take the Midwest out of the girl. I order up. For some strange reason, I even feel compelled to eat the potato chips with my sandwich, something I never, ever do.

Is it a latent expression of homesickness triggered by the disorienting circumstances of eating Western food while listening to Sting in a DNA pool of Hamites? Or does the tuna just look irresistibly tasty? Do the Egyptians who order it know how quintessentially American tuna salad is? Could it even be that some Egyptians have a passion for tuna fish salad the way that some Americans have a passion for Egyptian cotton? Or are tuna fish salad sales based strictly on novelty? Would the Egyptians who welcome tuna fish salad into their personal stomachs welcome us as readily into their collective homeland? Or, like the pirated DVDs of *Sex in the City* in the shop next door, did they want the symbol of America but not the real thing? Eyes, of course, follow us everywhere we go in the mall—hey! there's a couple of khawagaaya!—but we aren't quite as sensational in the mall as we are in the slum where we live. And I certainly feel more relaxed.

"Look!" I point to a storefront. "Sleeves."

Alex considers The Modesty Shop display. "Those sockie thingies?" He chuckles.

Muslim women, I explain, wear the sleeves under their veils in case they move an arm in such a way that the flesh above the glove is exposed. I also point out the dickies, those bizarre turtleneck garments with just enough fabric to make certain that the neck and throat stay covered, lest a woman move abruptly or loosen her veils in a sudden gust of wind. And then there are the stocking caps, which the women wear under the veils to make sure that no seductive lock of hair slips out of place. The black abaya goes over it all, unifying the parts in a continuous drape of black cloth. The facial veils are mostly simple transparent pieces of sheer black fabric, but the store also carries a kind of hockey-puck face-guard worn by ladies in Yemen. It makes them look very scary, at least to me.

"This is the place you go if you want to dress like a Muslim woman," I conclude.

"You aren't going to wear all this stuff, are you?" wonders Alex.

No way, I thought—once I get back to Europe, my cleavage is showing.

"Look at that one," says Alex. "Is she facing forward or backward?" We consider a manikin submerged in floes of black cloth. On the edge of the veils is a discrete row of black beading, matt, not shiny, since shiny things are considered haram under strict interpretations of Islamic law. "I can't see you wearing that," he says. "You look weird enough already."

He's not quite used to my Egyptian uniform yet.

"Alex—Egyptians think our clothes are weird, too. Here you don't judge women on how they look—here the women are all equal. And they hide Western clothes under their abayas if their husbands and fathers permit it. When they get home, they get rid of the veils and hang out in halter-tops and mini skirts.

"But why do they do that? Why put on all that stuff?" He is genuinely puzzled.

"Fabric or death," I announce.

1) Traditional Muslim women have to do what their husbands and fathers tell them; 2) The men have been taught at conservative mosques that there is a link between family honor and fabric; 3) In order to keep family honor intact, the men tell the women to wear fabric; and 4) If the women don't wear the fabric, wear it incorrectly, or bring dishonor upon the family in some other way, they can be killed. I don't tell Alex the part about being buried up to the neck in the earth and being publicly stoned, a fate Muslim women still suffer from Afghanistan to Algeria, though

more often a quick jab with a knife is preferred.

Alex suggests that maybe we should go into the store and buy me some extra layers, but I reassure him that as a foreign woman, I'm not being held to the same standards as my Egyptian sisters. I can't bring dishonor upon my family. Besides the lovely little boy whose hand slips so effortlessly into my own, I don't have one.

As long as I behave modestly, we'll be fine.

*****

In an adjacent bookstore, Alex flips through *The Magic School Bus* in Arabic, while I consult *Islamic Facts Refuting the Allegations against Islam* by Dr. Zakzouk. I go straight to the section on fashion. Dr. Zakzouk does not suffer from questions and confusions concerning Islamic dress. For him, the matter is clear:

"The attire that Islam imposes upon the Muslim woman is that she appears in a decent and respectable mien in order to save her from any unpleasant remarks or from being harassed by irresponsible youths or men. Thus the Muslim attire for women is to safeguard their honor and dignity and does not hinder their movement or activity. Islam does not command women to cover their faces with a veil or to wear gloves. This custom belongs to certain communities for which Islam is in no way responsible" (p. 74).

In other words, Islam does not advocate head-to-toe robes and veils, at least according to Dr. Zakzouk—it's the men running fundamentalist mosques. But like the American father who would tolerate a slightly low-cut blouse but prevent his teenage daughter from leaving the house in a transparent midriff, Dr. Zakzouk believes women should dress modestly for their own protection.

He's right.

I've never been in a hornier country.

*****

Every time I'm in Egypt, men offer to give me Muslim babies, a fact I've often pondered. In my experience, Greek men don't say, "You want Orthodox baby?" Japanese men don't say, "You want Shinto baby?" Even Jordanian, Syrian and Lebanese men don't proffer their seed, a couple of random Bedouin notwithstanding. But the phrase, "You want Muslim baby?" I've heard a lot in Egypt over the years, to the point that it no longer shocks me. Just the other day in the museum store in Cairo, a man asked if I'd like a Muslim child. "No thank you," I politely replied, as if I were declining a high-caloric sweet.

The Egyptian men who propose their semen aren't aggressive or rude. They're more like Boy Scouts, trying to do a good deed so they can get another badge. Their queries are gentle, rational, almost as if they feel sorry for me. In fact, I do think they feel sorry for me—a single woman, a single mom, clomping around their country, my maternal longing evidently stymied since I'm not tucked away taking care of the kids. But they'd never risk asking an Egyptian girl if she'd want a Muslim baby. No way.

"Look at it like this," a Greek diplomat to Egypt once explained. "Egyptian girls are virgins until they marry, and they keep the bloody sheets from the bed to prove it—sometimes the evidence is even examined by a Sheikh. If a girl is sexually wayward, she will never get married. She'll bring dishonor upon her family. They may ostracize her… or worse. Frankly, the behavior of some tourists here just reinforces the notion that Western women—"

"Are total sluts."

"Frankly, yes," the man agreed. "But the worst offender is the media. If you want your daughter to remain chaste until you find the right boy for her, how are you going to handle an episode of some sixth-rate US-made TV show portraying the sexual prowess of teenagers? You're going to think—thank God I don't live in that country among those people! And every time you see a Western woman on the streets of Egypt, you'll think she's like the show you saw last night."

Since the women in this land of tawny, dark-eyed beauties are kept under lock and key, the country is awash with repressed sexual energy that cannot manifest through flirtation, much less through physical touching or even autoeroticism. Islamic law confines sexual activity to marital intercourse or to the paradisiacal afterlife where 72 virgins will service each man, providing him with a "sensation," according to commentators, that is "out of this world." Virginity is obviously a key component in strict Muslim versions of satisfying orgasm. For reasons that remain obscure, Islamic sources equate sexual bliss with sexual ignorance.

At their origin, these rules for sexual behavior were aimed at groups of loosely affiliated tribes. When the Qur'an was codified, men married their first wife when they were 15, not 35 or 50. There wasn't a huge mass of disaffected youth, no seething urban centers, no gold standard. Where camel herders once reigned supreme, now horny young men, bursting with testosterone, simmer. In other countries, sexual longing is sublimated into jobs and hopes for the future. But there are no jobs in Egypt. Few men can obtain the minimum financial independence required for marriage. Few know the pleasure of god-given sexual release.

Into this raw void, where the longing of the soul screams and cries and whimpers, steps the Islamic fundamentalist agenda.

No wonder mainstreamers, like Dr. Zakzouk, are losing the battle. But I buy his book anyway. Then, true to my American upbringing, Alex and I march into the Carrefour Super-Center, determined to find a deal.

*****

It begins with a headache on the third day of school. "I need to lie down," says Alex.

I clutch a tepid mug of Nescafe, "Coffee American" as it's locally known. Alex and I have already had our breakfast—feta, pita and thumb bananas—and are about to meet the 6:45 AM mini van. "Are you sure you don't want to go to school?"

He nods, looking more confused than ill. After all, we've changed time zones, continents, languages, houses and schools in little over a week.

I hand him his coat. The to-do list pulses impatiently.

"Come on—you'll be OK."

I have a poem in my brain—I have to get it down before it flies away. Then I have to scavenge an internet connection, surmount bureaucracy at various agencies, meet with colleagues at the university and undertake the considerable labors of food shopping. I am determined to get a lot done.

Or so I think.

Something stops me from pushing my kid out the door.

*****

The screams from the golden couch are real. My son is in agony. It is the second time in his short life when he has suffered the kind of excruciating pain that adults seldom forget. I wish I could die myself, transfer that pain from him to me, take it, all of it, in some sort of wretched intravenous transfer that would save him from the onslaught of misery. Oily tears smear his face, his temperature just over 40C/104F and, like the burning star in the morning sky, climbing.

"Mommy's going to help you," I say calmly, trying to hide my fear, my egregious ineptitude, my flat uncertainty as to where, exactly, Mommy might find help.

*****

Four years ago. We are in Beirut. All of a sudden, like one of the Israeli bombs exploding too close to home, Alex is in crucifying pain—he actually passes out from the pain. I think he is dying. I call a friend to help me translate at the hospital, and she says I must call Dr. Ayoub. "Now!" she admonishes. "Dawn, call him now!" She knows the country better than I do. While my son lingers in an ashen state, the film of death upon his face, I dial—it's a rotary phone, so I have to place my finger carefully. Get it in the number slot, slide it around. The doctor tells me to hail a cab and bring Alex to his house. "Hospital! Hospital!" I scream into the phone because I think my son is dying. I can still hear the doctor's words: "Madame, you will regret taking your child to the hospital. I suggest you bring him to me first."

All the way to Dr. Ayoub, I watch my son die—he is unresponsive, then screaming, then unresponsive. I hold him in my arms while the clock slows, slows to a pace that only crisis allows one to perceive, when you realize that so much of what takes up your life, your attention, takes you away from all that matters, the present moment, one breath, and then another.

The doctor greets us wearing a silk dressing gown. We walk past a small, original Monet painting hanging in his living room—I glimpse it the way one notices a flower in a devastated landscape—and go to the examining room. No words are exchanged. The doctor looks Alex over while I lean against a wall, weeping. After a while, he says quite simply, "Your son will live." Later, we arrive at the hospital to meet the surgeon Ayoub has summoned for the procedure. Alex is limp in my arms. The two urgent care interns, who Ayoub has prompted to receive us, are intently reading *The Pediatric Guide to Emergency Medicine*. I see it in one doctor's hand, the other one reading over his shoulder.

I don't let them touch Alex until the surgeon arrives.

*****

There is no Dr. Ayoub to call in Alexandria. My infrastructure isn't sketched yet, let alone the girders of a network. There is no ambulance to call, no paramedics. The Fulbright staff in Cairo won't be at their desks for another hour or so. They haven't supplied me with a list of emergency contacts because they don't have them. And even if they had them, the numbers change, the phones go out, the line ends up in a store where everyone wants to help but no one understands what you're saying.

Once a woman I barely knew, a woman who lives in New York City, a mother of two small children, reproached me for not having a pediatrician before leaving for Egypt or Lebanon or wherever. She didn't understand. So much she didn't understand.

Alexandria is not America. Alexandria is not Cairo. There are no detailed maps or phonebooks in any language. Ditto a directory service. Scant expatriate resources. Guidebooks exist in honor of the glorious city that Alexander the Great founded, but no guidebooks to demystify the scruffy modern one. If you need something, it's phone-tree all the way. If the phones work.

My landlady Fatima doesn't answer hers. The switchboard at Alex's school isn't on yet. I can knock on a neighbor's door in the General Tower 13 with an English-Arabic glossary in hand. But which door will open on the path of knowledge, expert medical care, relief? Who can I turn to in Alexandria? The only thing I'm sure of is that I have to know exactly where—or to whom—I'm taking him.

Alex screams.

I stand in the emergency of my life.

Nazek! The Chair of the English Department at Alexandria University!

Knowing things is a scholar's business.

"German Hospital!" Nazek shouts into the phone in an effort to make herself heard over Alex's cries.

I half-carry my son to the elevator. But in my fluster I have forgotten to ring the soldier on the interphone before I close the door. I have to drag Alex back, open the door to the apartment, and shout into the interphone: MIDFADLUK! ASANSAYAR! TALATTASHAR!

The soldier sends the elevator up and calls it back down—the only way it functions. As we descend, we view the club sandwich of floor doors and floor insulation—sometimes with wires, sometimes with pipes, and often with crunchy stuff I hope isn't asbestos. The elevator itself has no door.

"MOTASHFA ALMANEE," I roar into the lobby. The soldier's eyes widen in alarm.

"Monsieur-Madame—!" He scoops Alex up and surges down the broken sidewalk, past abandoned vehicles full of cats, to the street to hail a cab. Just the other day, Alex and I stopped at one of the cars where we thought the cats were dead. We rapped on the windows. They moved.

By the time we reach the hospital, Alex's pain has, like a sudden thunderstorm, ceased. He can hold himself upright, unassisted. The aspirin I've given him has kicked in, and his fever has fallen. I don't know what worries me more—his capricious symptoms or the medical consultation. After all, the reason Alex got so sick in Beirut was that a doctor from the best hospital in Lebanon misdiagnosed his illness.

*****

Hospitals that serve the poor are always under-funded, whether they're in the projects of Detroit or the center of Paris. The German Hospital in Alexandria is no exception. Judging by the crowd at the soiled entrance, the ubiquitous trash mounding the steps, money isn't available to staff it properly, let alone repair the cracked walls or repaint. I wonder what the hospitals are like that care for Egyptians who cannot afford even a nominal consulting fee.

The crowd looks at us and parts. The sick, the maimed, the pained, the disfigured, the suffering—they let us pass. I want to wait, to take our turn—I feel unworthy of the privilege, as if that blond hair is being treated like real gold. Did some weird colonial reflex, something left over from the British occupation, open a path through the masses? Or was it more of a class issue than a racial one, since by definition we are rich Anglos and they poor Egyptians? Or is it the sickly look on my son's face? The worry that inscribes mine? These conflicting emotions pale in the presence of my fear. My only concern is saving my son from more pain.

The nurse who greets us in Urgent Care wears immaculate white veils that frame the moon of her face. She has an admirable command of English. I recount Alex's symptoms. She eyes him skeptically. "No fever," she says, pressing a perfectly manicured hand to his forehead. I am relieved to see her fingernails are impeccably clean.

"But fever very high! Fever 40.3." I insist, pointing to my watch. "One hour ago, fever high. Much pain here!" I point to my stomach.

"Diarrhea?"

"No." I can't help pointing to my bottom—when I'm in sign-language mode, it's difficult to stop. "Here, OK."

She leads us to a cubicle with a bed covered with a clean sheet. Various old, sad, outdated medical apparati stand guard around the parameter, like ancient retainers of a prior medical regime. The walls are soiled with the gloom of illness and tragedy.

"How are you feeling, Sweet Pea?"

The bags under Alex's eyes, translucent silver shadows, whisper in the florescent light. Then the pain hit. He folds into a torturous work of origami, moaning.

"MIDFADLUK!" I yell, yanking the curtain, noting that I'd promised myself not to touch it. The nurse runs back, her face whitening with alarm. "I see."

While she summons the doctor, I hold Alex in my arms, feeling a kind of fear I had felt in Beirut, when the one you love more than anything else in the entire world, the one you love more than yourself, the one you want to teach, and help, and nourish, and protect, is powerless in the throes of suffering, and all you can do is touch and hold and rock and reassure when really and truly, if you are honest, you only want someone else to touch and hold and rock and reassure you.

"I here," a young man in casual dress announces. "I Doctor. What problem?"

He is a cheerful fellow emanating confidence. I trust him immediately, although I have no rational reason for doing so. "Here," I say. "Here problem."

A tucked and grimacing Alex points at the upside-down V-shape below his ribcage.

The pain halts as abruptly as it has commenced. The doctor runs his hand lightly over Alex's abdomen in a practiced gesture that has always seemed to me more intuitive than empirical. Then he pulls a plastic glove full of tongue depressors from his back pocket—obviously a private stash—and peers into Alex's throat with such determination that Alex gags and chokes.

"There it!" he exclaims, breaking the tongue depressor in two and lobbing it triumphantly into the trash. "I doctor university, pediatric medicine."

"I doctor university, too. Literature."

"Alexandria University?"

I nod.

We pause a split-second in mutual recognition before entering into a lengthy noun-driven communication.

The doctor explains that Alex has contracted a serious bacterial infection called haemophilus influenza. It comes with a high fever, manifests in the throat and drips down into the stomach, triggering excruciating abdominal pain. Antibiotics are prescribed. Then the injection.

Who cares what the hospital looks like—this guy knows what he's doing.

"Stop now," he concludes solemnly, referring both to his imminent departure and to the healing properties of what proved to be a large, burning shot in Alex's hip.

I pay the equivalent of $2.00 and leave with medications, precise instructions on food and drink, and an admonition to phone every four hours. I think the doctor is perhaps overly solicitous in having me check in so often. It's only later that I learn haemophilus influenza is the precursor to meningitis.

It's the primary school nurse who tells me. "I have to go through all the immunization records in the school to make sure the other children Alex came in contact with are immunized," she says sternly. "The children from Saudi Arabia and the Emirates are legally required to have HIB vaccinations, and the Egyptian parents are very good about it, too. It's the children who were vaccinated in Europe and America that I have to be careful about."

I don't understand why Alex wasn't immunized—his pediatrician examined him and gave him a tetanus booster before departure. I also don't understand how Alex could have become infected so fast—after all, we've barely arrived. But there are moments of life in which so much happens that time itself seems to dilate, and you live more intensely in the span of a few days than you have in last few months, or even years.

Egypt always has that effect on me.

MARGINALIA ON MARGINALISM IN CONTEMPORARY TIMES

by Ömer Gökçümen and Radu Iovitza

There is a lot to ignore today. Cultural noise—advertising, movies, news, e-mails, music—comes in a constant stream. Not all need, or should, be ignored—but it must be dealt with. But what connections in this cacophony have true social consequence? Take three events: at a college party, a young man wearing a Che Guevara t-shirt is talking to a girl wearing an East German army coat; a well-known Russian mathematician refuses, and subsequently hides in his mother's apartment, from the highest honour in mathematics; a famous French philosopher who is also a public intellectual refuses the Nobel Prize in Literature and sends a letter to an important newspaper explaining why he did so. The last two seem, at first glance, to be parallel, and the first to be a different beast entirely. But look closer at their socially recognizable meaning and a common pattern emerges. In particular, in this essay we'd like to explore the theme of self-definition by individuals and groups through acts that relegate them to a social minority–a process we call "marginalism." As we go through and analyse various aspects of this question, we'd like you to keep these three examples in mind.

Who's in, and who's out—maybe more importantly, who's on the border and what to do with them? These questions are fundamental to the dynamics of any human social system. Millions of such calculations are performed at dizzying speeds by every individual each day. Some are ephemeral and situational—as in an office or family dispute or at a party—whereas others are relatively stable and marshal the forces of thousands of people, such as structures that govern labour or political organizations. For that reason we document their properties and histories, and we assign moral values to various examples.

Pre-modern accounts of society ignored the marginal elements within it. Nomads, illiterate peasants, gangsters, transvestites, homosexuals, women—none benefited from documentation. Some couldn't write or didn't care to, others were, and perhaps still are, too secretive or dangerous for ethnographers and historians to venture near. They are difficult to document because either they do not signal their presence or their signals are lost or misunderstood. Perhaps out of scientific curiosity, perhaps as a result of a desire for fairness, social sciences in the modern era have paid a great deal of attention to marginal elements—those aspects of societies which had been "invisible." Today, "marginal" and "marginality" are popular and relatively often-encountered words not only in academic but also within journalistic discourses. But are all these referring to the same concept? What exactly is a marginal person? A marginal group? A marginal idea? How do individuals or groups take advantage of the margin, the edge, the border, to redefine themselves?

MARGINAL vs. MARGINALIZED

The folk understanding of marginality associates being "at the edge" with the pitiable condition of those pushed away from the core of society on the one hand, and with a certain elusive and desirable quality found in progressive free-thinkers on the other. In other words, marginal status can be created consciously, or it can be forced on one by others. Thus, the quality of the marginal condition depends on how one became marginal in the first place.

Marcos's statement on his own identification with the world's marginalized people, and, for that matter, virtually any Marxist world-view, is based on a view of marginalism as an essentially passive condition. It is imposed by elites on the masses in order to produce advantages for themselves. But the Zapatista leader also highlights some interesting cases which essentially consist of people who are simply disconnected—housewives, artists without galleries, journalists writing fillers for the back pages, and Communists in a capitalist world. People are often lonely in the midst of others, and this has nothing to do with being economically or socially exploited, at least not consciously. Nobody profits from the isolation and the oft-quoted alienation of lonely housewives or unsuccessful artists. And yet, we can see parallels between these kinds of marginals and Communists after the Cold War—namely in a certain dissonance with the surrounding discourse.

Keeping this in mind, we'd like to draw attention to a case of weakness turned to strength. In 1964, Jean-Paul Sartre refused the Nobel Prize for literature, arguing that the writer should not be affiliated with any institutions, and causing an international scandal. Few would dare to argue that the philosopher was a humble man—but humility has nothing to do with refusing recognition and fame, because rejecting such a prize results in absolute notoriety. Had Sartre refused a small local French prize, he would at best have appeared ungrateful—the bigger the opposition, the more important one becomes. In fact, because membership to such powerful status-defined social groups, such as the community of Nobel laureates, has such a high rate of acceptance, the act of deliberately and publicly refusing to become a member has enormous status-producing rewards for the dissenter, or for the group he represents (in the case of Sartre, "writers"). Thus, in fact, Sartre, but not the writer in general, becomes less marginalized and, ironically, more central, by performing a marginal act. More specifically, in the moment when a central character redefines his position as marginal, he effectively shifts the center to the margin, and vice-versa.

Reinventing oneself as "marginal" as a useful strategy for success is not restricted to individuals like Sartre, who claim to be representing a group, but is often employed by ctual groups, such as the ubiquitous and quite mainstream teenage punks or goths. Any individual has the opportunity to appeal to the notion of marginality in the desired field of action, without having to actually step outside the mainstream in other aspects of his or her life. For instance, one can at the same time claim to be a marginal as a humanistic intellectual in an unimaginative and overly businesslike society and yet remain a perfectly normal consumer of capitalist goods and a well-paid writer in other aspects of life.

This is not to say that claiming marginality is hypocritical or immoral—it is a social strategy like any other. Nevertheless, in order to exploit the power of difference and dissension, cultural models that describe the dichotomy of being in and out of the system must already exist and be available for the public to examine. In Sartre's case, the idea that humanism is being lost at the expense of political and economic interests and that the writer's condition is threatened already existed for a long time.

But what happens then when such cultural models are not already in place? This is the truly interesting case of what we will call "true" marginals, those who cannot reference frameworks of societal understanding for their position.

TRUE MARGINALISM

The person living truly "on the edge" of society cannot be identified—exactly because cultural categories relating to this condition are lacking. This makes the perfect true marginal, a hypothetical and essentially impossible social being. By default, the condition of being truly marginal is idiosyncratic and cannot be known by mainstream society for the time of its existence. In other words, true marginalism is not of the present, but of the past or future.

Even for groups, the actualization and definition of the marginal condition can happen simply through an interaction with mainstream discourse. Take for instance the beginnings of a nation-state. Discourses related to the process of nation-building often incorporate definitions of ethnic or national identities, which, in turn, results in majority ethnic groups and minorities, as well as groups that are entirely outside the "ethnic" framework. In the case of the Gypsies of Eastern Europe, a place where nation-building resulted from 19th-century ideas related to language, religion, and the land, the Gypsy peripatetic and culturally chameleonic social structure excluded them from the system. They could not be a "proper" ethnic group like their neighbours: Serbs, Czechs, Romanians, Hungarians, etc. One hundred and fifty years later, the idea of ethnicity and the concept of majority and minority within the nation-state has fully penetrated mainstream discourse—and only nowadays are Gypsies beginning to apply such cultural terms to their own groups in order to benefit from various advantages offered by national governments.

Many other examples could be given with respect to groups that today draw their identities from ethnicity, race, sexual orientation, and other social categories. In general, groups can drift in and out of a marginal position depending on the availability of changing categories for dividing up the full behavioral spectrum. But occasionally, they are able to interfere with this process of drift and actually bring about either acceptance or exclusion, depending on the desired outcome.

MINORITY GAMES

The French post-structural anthropologist Pierre Bourdieu discusses the uses of a differentiating mechanism—the accepted dichotomy of high culture and popular culture for instance—by various societal subgroups in order to gain status and privilege. In Bourdieu's concept of distinction, cultural elites are constituted through differentiation from the mainstream in conjunction with their ability to attract elements within the mainstream to participate in elite activities. For instance, members of the commercial classes perceive going to the opera or attending avant-garde art openings as conferring upon them an aura of distinction and superiority, despite the fact that their own tastes would naturally align elsewhere. Where our argument on marginalism departs from Bourdieu's is that the *a priori* distinction that marks different classificatory categories is in fact a universal motor behind social alignment.

If a classificatory dichotomy is already present—and these dichotomies can be simple, as in dark-light, or complex, such as bohemian-bourgeois—it can be picked up irrespective of its intrinsic properties, and manipulated in such a way that the category that is less frequent becomes the desirable one. Recent experiments with heterosexual male subjects' preference for hair color in women showed that men often prefer the color that is least frequent. However, in our case, we are more interested in pursuing an explanation of minority behavior. This kind of phenomenon is very frequently observed in fashion trends—where clothing styles and haircuts are explicitly linked to circulating notions of taste, decency, sexuality, and political orientation.

For a less obvious example, let us pick sport. Today, sport, and especially team sport, is hailed not only as an important part of the physical regime required for good health, but also as character-building and useful for teaching young people cooperation and teamwork. In this case, sport is linked to the discourse that dichotomizes people in sportive/active/cooperative/rugged on the one hand, and fat/lazy/selfish/soft on the other. Given the current state of both physical and mental health in many Western industrialized societies, this dichotomy puts the practitioners of team sports in the minority. But it was not always so. In the popular 16th-century etiquette book *The Courtier*, Baldassare Castiglione describes team sports such as rugby as "beastlie furye" practiced by the common people and unfit for a gentleman. In Castiglione's context, the dichotomy is class-based. By definition almost, those involved in individual sports such as fencing, running, and swimming were the aristocrats, and team games were for the peasants to amuse themselves communally. In this case, the former are seen as individualistic/strong/refined and the peasants as communal/brutish/rough. Again, by default, this dichotomy, which, in the case of *The Courtier,* is partly a result of self-justification on the part of the ruling classes, puts the minority in poll position.

The object of the above example is not to demonstrate the cultural relativity of sport as a concept, but to show that any dichotomy can be exploited either way, so long as those who are in the minority are regarded as superior. Thus, what is cultural and completely relative is the classificatory framework itself and the distinction it proposes, and what is universal is the frequency preference we describe here as marginalism.

The essential quality that gives power to a minority group is simply marking within discourse. The presence of extra-symbolic associations with a group attracts attention and suggests that the group follows a different social strategy from that of the mainstream. The crucial element is that marking implies a frequency that is not negligible—or else it would go by unnoticed—yet is less than the rest of the central group. It suggests stability at low frequency, which in turn means that the success of the strategy and the frequency of players are inextricably linked. Such frequency-dependent selection types occur in nature all the time, and the ability to correctly mark or signal the difference is an essential part of making the strategy work. It must be noted however, that taking advantage of minority marking within pre-existing discursive frameworks is actually a privilege—simply having access to a large enough variety of discursive forms in order to be able to manipulate them is a considerable advantage. Conversely, lacking such access constitutes one of the main reasons why individuals with non-standard social strategies are often truly marginal in the sense discussed here.

THAT OBSCURE OBJECT OF IDENTITY—OR, HOW TO EXPLOIT THE DANGER OF MARGINALISM

Let us return to the Sartre example: imagine that Sartre had been a chemist or a biologist. Intellectual independence stands at the roots of Western academia, yet no one would even so much as recognize the logic in a chemist's refusal of the Nobel Prize on grounds of independence. Why is this? Simply because the institution of Science is not in the least threatened or 'marginalized' in contemporary Western culture. On the contrary, it is hegemonic. Sartre is, in fact, wrenching the humanities, and in particular, the arts, out of the framework of the academic world of results, dissemination, and reformulation. In essence, this act is exploiting an existing binary distinction that is rarely taken seriously in intellectual circles, and exaggerating its terms in order to achieve an extreme position, where a prize turns into an insult. As outcasts, writers are neither accountable to the Swedish Academy, nor to the U. S. National Science Foundation, nor to the Soviet Government, nor to Hollywood producers. From being useless members of society, they become dangerous possessors of ultimate freedom. Self-defined outcasts are scary and unpredictable—and it is exactly those qualities that can be exploited in order to gain influence. As the French philosopher Jacques Derrida stated in a 1989 piece with a colossal title ("Some Statements and Truisms about Neologisms, Newisms, Postisms, Parasitisms, and other small Seismisms"): "Monsters cannot be announced. One cannot say: 'here are our monsters,' without immediately turning the monsters into pets."

The best recent example of this is the media exploitation of the famous German cannibal case, which is one of the most esoteric acts to be publicized in the last few years. Armin Meiwes and Bernd Jürgen Brandes met on the internet, and Brandes agreed to be killed and eaten by Meiwes. It is almost as impossible to imagine how anyone could accept such a proposal, as it is impossible to understand how Meiwes sat down at the dinner table and shared with his victim the latter's cooked penis. However, the incident immediately caught media attention, and rather than the actual act and the true inclinations of Brandes and Meiwes, it was immediately reproduced through media elements, such as the song "Mein Teil," which would translate into *my part* or *my penis*, by the German metal group Rammstein. By integrating a completely marginal act to their music making, they immediately transformed the cannibalism of Brandes to a consumable, non-marginal, cultural product.

We said earlier that we would not expect scientists to refuse recognition in the same way as Sartre. And yet, a little more than a year ago, a Russian mathematician, Grigori Perelman, refused the Fields Medal—mathematics's Nobel Prize. However, unlike Sartre, he not only refused the official recognition, the prize, but also refused publicity. He does not talk to the press, lives with his mother, has returned to work for an institute in Russia for very little money and he seems to be sincere in his attitude. Still, the media continue to exploit his story, forcing him into the stereotype of the marginal crazy scientist genius—and neither he nor any group of like-minded individuals are profiting from this. In this case, we might be dealing with a real marginal—one whose actions are incongruent with currently available discourse. Whatever Dr. Perelman's motives may be, our point is not to make speculations about them, but to give him as an example of the iconization of marginal behavior.

Individuals or groups on the road to self-definition as marginal often rely on an easily recognizable and often exaggerated iconism in order to make the marking stand out. It is not a coincidence that most of these stereotyped marginal symbols, behaviors and actions are distorted copies of their true marginal counterparts—many of which were responsible for significantly offending mainstream society. Violent acts, sexual immorality, cultural and economic disturbance immediately draw attention—but not all press is good press. In a world of symbolic overload, it is far easier to substitute a token in order to affiliate oneself with a movement or a group.

Take, for instance, Communism and the image of Che Guevara. Within American society, actually subverting the capitalist machine and advocating the dictatorship of the proletariat is considered at best ideologically alien and at worst downright dangerous. But Che is also a handsome and dreamy idealist physician at the same time as a murderous Communist revolutionary. This is partly responsible for his public notoriety in comparison with, say, Fidel Castro or Kim Jong–Il, neither of which appears on college students' t-shirts nearly as often as Che. The compatibility of Che's image with a score of young idealist would-be world-changers, both real and fictional, permits those who wish to vaguely affiliate themselves with politically radical marginals to employ this kind of iconism. But the process is a two-way street—the effect is on both sides—Che is nowadays taken less seriously as a revolutionary, and the bearers of Che t-shirts are, as per their own desire, understood as playful mavericks of mainstream society. The irony behind the commercialization of Che's image perfectly illustrates the process we have repeatedly mentioned, namely the distortion and reinvention of the marginal identity as a minority within the mainstream.

THE MARGINAL INTELLECTUAL —PRODUCT OF IDENTITY POLITICS IN ACADEMIA?

This essay itself brewed within the basic fear of being "out." We, the writers of this piece, identify ourselves as intellectuals, and we are trapped between an obsession to differentiate ourselves from the general public—simply because we want to be recognized as intellectuals—and, at the same time remain a relevant group. The intellectual pursuit is increasingly evaluated by its relevance to immediate contemporary issues, especially within American public discourse. Thus, despite the fact that the marginality of intellectuals is indeed a myth, intellectuals are losing their identity as a self-defined group and are being redefined by public opinion. The reason we are not heard is because of our failure to engage with the popular discourse and because of our own dissonance within public discourse. We are understood only when "intellectualism" is "in" or relevant to contemporary political concerns.

Last year, Senator Kay Bailey Hutchison (R-TX), chair of a panel that oversees the National Science Foundation, the U.S.-government-funded agency that sets up and distributes funds for scientific research, asked the following rather blunt question to the Director of the NSF: "Why is the National Science Foundation (NSF) funding a study of a women's cooperative in Bangladesh?...Why are U.S. taxpayers footing the bill for efforts to understand Hungary's emerging democracy? . . . And why are social scientists even bothering to compile an archive of state legislatures in a long-gone era when those legislators chose U.S. senators?" She proposed later to cease funding for certain social science departments, such as anthropology and political science.

She even suggested the expulsion from the NSF of fields such as anthropology. However, part of the reason why she did not find the results she was looking for was exactly due to our refusal as intellectuals to explain what we do to the greater public.

Thus, whether or not we believe James Atlas, the marginality of the intellectual within academia and of academia itself within the realm of human productivity is an acute problem today in most industrialized societies. When intellectuals allowed knowledge production to be subsumed within production in the broader sense, they did not realize that they would one day be judged according to very unfamiliar criteria.

For our own selfish reasons we have allowed the public to construct the ivory-tower metaphor, and to consider us elites. More importantly, we, in anthropology, have allowed other sciences to be misinformed about what we do, and we have not strived to create connections with things that concern others in other fields. American academia then has become a kind of strange space of marginalism—where the humanities and arts continue to exist largely because they have made a successful pass at defining themselves as marginal with respect to the sciences. But, as the social sciences and humanities continue to distance themselves from the public and ever-growing relevance of "hard sciences" to the global discourse, they slowly became truly marginal—in true dissonance with all other discourses. This is a hardly enviable position—but one cannot help wondering if we have not ourselves created this dissonance in the above-mentioned process of self-promotion.

Voluntarily trapped in our Ivory Towers, which, once conceived and perceived as mysterious and complex have been redefined by society as alien, elitist, and snobbish, we are now nerdy at best, sometimes arrogant, and, worst of all, irrelevant. But as the battle for relevance rages on, all hope is not lost. As Michel Foucault once observed (via Didier Eribon):

"There are more ideas on earth than intellectuals imagine. And these ideas are more active, stronger, more resistant, and more passionate than "politicians" think. We have to be there at the birth of ideas, the bursting outward of their force: not in books expressing them, but in events manifesting this force, in struggles carried on around ideas, for or against them. Ideas do not rule the world. But it is because the world has ideas (and because it constantly produces them) that it is not passively ruled by those who are its leaders or those who would like to teach it, once and for all, what it must think."

LAST WORDS

We have tried to describe the process by which socially marginal entities, from individuals to large groups, arise, are picked up by the ever-changing mainstream discourse, and eventually institutionalized socially, culturally, and, last but not least, economically. We do not wish to paint a depressing picture of true counter-cultural innovation being eaten up and iconized in Hollywood movie posters that adorn the windows of every world cinema—marginal thoughts, ideas, individuals, and groups, are not simply safe pockets of controlled anti-culture, but also serve the essentially creative function of defining the boundaries of the mainstream.

RESURRECTED MANHUNT

by Willie Smith

Find myself once again back in 1969, hunting rhino downtown. Have swallowed a couple PCP tabs.

What you do is sneak up on one peeing. Pour salt on his tail. He'll freeze long enough for you to saw off the horn, grind it into powder, cap it up. Sell it down in Chinatown for hardon medication.

Sometime after midnight I locate one urinating against a lamp post. Creep up. Salt rhino back. Pull out the hack. Saw the camel out of his throat. Rush home.

But as I'm about to feed the beast into the grinder, he snakes his head around; begs for his life. Says if I spare him he'll tell me a story can hypnotize girls into bed.

"How do I know it'll work?"

"How do I know," he chews sideways a moment, "if I tell the story you'll let me go?"

I shrug. Contemplate the bound ruminant. Quite the conundrum. This a job for drugs.

I light a cigarette. Inhale. Nicotine clears the head. Tar makes me a tad more dead.

"OK, here's what: I step outta the room. You tell it on tape. I re-enter. Take the tape, go hang out in the park. Play it back the first dish happens along. If she says 'Ah,' spreads her legs, lets me mount—when I orgasm, the harmonics'll key into my cell a code that releases the cuffs, leg irons, anklets, choke collar, so forth."

"And this'll make sure," the camel with his muzzle types into my cell a virus would take Gates himself two decades to quarantine, "you don't block sending the code."

I exhale. I wouldn't trust me either.

Catch the redeye to Volunteer. That's a Seattle park. May as well bleed there as anywhere. 69 was a spooky, albeit boring, year. And the rhino tranq has warped me all over the Turkey from Agnew to Clinton. I knew who to vote; just not where; everywhere seems to be choosing at once.

Slip into a bucket. Gobble another peace pill. Step out. Occupy a bench beside the gem of a toilet.

Because it is dark, disinfectant issuing like McDonald's overriding shit stink from the latrine, and because the bladder is for the moment leaving me alone, decide to meditate—to kill time in a vegetarian sort of way. I never kill anything with a face.

Visualize sideways 69—symbol for Cancer the crab, who walks sideways, according to French wives, because he is perpetually masturbating; also visualizing, of course, mutual-face-sitting. Face it: only difference between meditation and masturbation is a couple letters and a decision as to which end is going to decide.

Cancer rolls over into the year Kerouac croaked. Jack walks sideways in an alley. Not down, not up; just in. Bounces off sooty walls at a rate of five butts a minute. Now and then compounding the sideways gait with a stumble forward or a lurch back.

Kerouac seems trapped in this alley. I look around for Virgil. Spy only madness and bedpans. Close eyes. Darkness.

Wrench myself up onto the moon. From there—inside Clavius—crater the movie 2001 makes famous—I observe Viet Nam on TV lurch forward, stumble back, while apparently on way too much acid.

My cousin Chuck the paratrooper lights a joint. Slips out into the stream. Hangs his plummeting guts a mile above a paddy. Dark there, too. He fights Communism at night. By day he is a heroin addict on the outskirts of Saigon.

Then this girl comes sits down. Her bouquet of opium, bath salts, spearmint gum, rum & coke, scatters the disinfectant I've been getting used to.

"Don't tell me," I say into the night. "It's Goldie Hawn."

"Don't be silly," she says. "Got a cigarette?"

"I quit." Pull the pack out of my shirt. Flip her a pall mall.

"Sorry," I say. "Look, here's a tape I gotta play ya—'K?"

I've already got the thing going, the reel reeling, and this baritone, a Charles Kurrault knockoff, says, "I've got a gun in my pocket. Listen to what I say or I blow your tits off."

She starts blubbering, begging for her rotten little bitch life, and she ain't even married. I smack her around. Torture is OK now in America, so what the fuck, I put some water on, intending to make soup in her snatch. Spigoting kettle, I realize we must be back at my apartment. Look around instinctively for the camel. Or was that his place?

Stare into the muzzle of what looks like a .38. My .38. She must've found it in my top drawer, where I always keep the sucker loaded, oiled, good to go. I'd forgotten, you see, that she was not the camel, so was not tied up like a coffin nail. Not tied up at all.

"Unzip your pants and hold out your dick," the copycat Kurrault barks. "I want to see how a pecker looks over the site of this fat pistol. I don't know much about guns, but I have in my day shot a few dicks off."

"Don't do it, lady," I beg, stalling, astonished at how the tape is speaking through Iris's lips, tongue, throat. It seems "Kurrault" has shanghaied her vocal apparatus. "They hang murderers in this state!"

She grins. "Now how do you come to know my name is Iris?"

I stare into her irises. Think back—two bees jostling chartreuse irises. Messenger of Hera… did I *say* Iris?

The queen speaks, disguised as bigbelly Kurrault. Orders Iris to fly over the rainbow, pump the reds out of Judy Garland, get her to singing again; turn everybody from a rhinoceros into a stock broker.

"But what about poetry?" Iris weeps, gun trembling in fist. "What have you hunters done? Do you really think a single anthem by the US air force will twist anxiety back into the fate we ate for meat during the Truman administration—when there was no true man in the whole whorehouse!"

I suggest the camel stop exaggerating. Fish a fresh pack of luckies from my bottom drawer, keeping hands up, except to dive the right into the drawer, come up with the pack. I feed her a butt. Strike a match. Light another serif into her death warrant.

"Thanks," she says, shooting the dick I've been holding in my hand all this time off.

No pain at first. Just like they say. But blood everywhere. Somewhere they say that, too. Iris the camel crashes through the wall. I don't know how I ever forgot her name. Iris is my mother's name.

You can picture how all this kinda scarred me. I have no one to blame but myself. Yes, it's my fault, officer. All my fault. But I swear—I swear to you on my mother's anus—I did not kill me.

"Then who did?" Kurrault purrs.

"I think it was…" the bee inside my iris hovers (time is, time was, listen to the bee buzz)… "that rhino down on skid row."

"The one you rolled? The street drunk you sawed up into pieces for one lousy cigarette?"

"No," I hang my head, focus on a baby roach waddling across the blotter. "It was the camel. I gave the camel to Iris. The rest is history."

"Except you didn't. You gave Iris a pall mall."

"Isn't that an alley in London?" I wink at the pinhead insect.

The gun belches. Apparently she fired. To the floor the camel drops. (That's how forest fires get started). If Iris is my mother, does that make the queen my godgranddam?

Baffled, I die—riding bareback succeeding nightmares.

JOIN THE CULT OF WILLIE SMITH

"If James Joyce had wanted to write like Dashiell Hammett, and had a sense of humor, he would have written like Willie Smith."

—*Reflex Magazine*

Willie Smith has been a long-time contributor to the *Corpse*. Back in the 90s, he used to send us actual manual typewriter-written stories, after everyone else had made the switch to computers. We didn't press Willy to get on the email, though, because there were always loads of crazy manic violent humor to look forward to in the random envelopes that kept filling up old PO Box 25051. This was back before the government allowed people to own their own scanners, so we always had to take Willie's stories to the Scanning Dept. at the university, where Rush Limbaugh played all day long and the ladies were quite exasperated at having to get up out of their seats and take Willie's work to the machine. And after they got a look at the content (ie, Jesus getting beat up in modern-day Seattle, sex with a giant arachnid, etc.), they were even less thrilled to convert our literary luddite's narratives into MS Word. In fact, those ladies even lodged a complaint against the *Corpse,* claiming that we "sexually harassed" them by creating a hateful working environment.

But that's the thing about Willie: if you don't have a sense of humor, he will irritate the hell out of you. Just take his story "Spider Fuck," for example, published in issue #9 of the *Cyber Corpse*. As legend has it, Willie read this story at Naropa and sent half the audience scrambling for the door so as not to vomit. In Willie's own words:

"The crowd at Naropa seemed to enjoy my reading; but it was my second reading of this story (I've never read it in toto since) over the Labor Day weekend of 1995 at Seattle's annual art/music festival Bumbershoot that provoked outrage and even (sigh!) my first publically printed death threat. Danny Housman, then music editor of *The Stranger,* a Seattle alternative weekly then only a few years old, wasted a good two columns of ink lambasting my reading. 'I wouldn't mind cutting off Willie Smith's oxygen supply,' the article, to the best of my memory, began. Danny ended by accusing me of being 'a giant asshole,' which I thought a gross exaggeration. I'm really a rather runt-of-the-litter sort of asshole. But it is possible that my Naropa reading of 'Spider Fuck' did not go over well with the powers that be, as I was never asked back; or maybe that's just because of my relative invisibility; people often complain they can never find me, never find anything about me. This seems to be my fate. Cult of anonymity indeed."

That last line refers to an article entitled "Cult of Anonymity," written by Fred Moody of the *Seattle Weekly,* in which he states: "Smith is an ambitious ne'er-do-well who enjoys—or, to judge from the way he reacts to accolades, endures—a considerable cult following in Seattle." Willie takes issue with this claim, but there's no disputing the fact that his novel *Oedipus Cadet,* published in 1990 by Black Heron Press, has become a cult classic. So culty, in fact, that Jesse Bernstein wrote "Willie Smith has a reason for writing that goes hand in hand with my reason for reading: surviving under a crushing weight by proving daily that it is not a crushing weight. This writing is the only kind of argument that beats universal inertia. Heads roll here."

Meanwhile, Willie and his cult are still in Seattle, where he continues to provoke the deadpan masses. Having chucked his ancient Smith & Carona, he's made the quantum leap to YouTube, where you can see him performing his knee-slapping prose by searching for wsmith49. Check out "How the Cops Fixed my Ass" and prepare to laugh your own right off (ms).

BEATITUDES & INTERSTICITIES

by Dave Brinks

ROSE OF THE TRANS-STIGMATAS

BEATITUDE THE FIRST

back when I was an old child
barely biblical and
the monkeys perched on my eyelids
were still colostruming
not quite 48,000 stellar bursts from Pangaea
slightly more than 3,000,000 parsecs
from goat herding & polyandry
that my heart was no paper Judas
but a shiny evil pot of goo
immensely turtled in its reality
moldy spells of duende
what cloven-hoof smells what phlegm craves
how could I let you get away, Tiamat
was I not legion enough in my head
was I not equal in cupidity & contumely
who gave spawn to Great Marduk
and fearful as you might be
of his stinky breath & unmatched guile
lacerate his ears I will, in public
and in private, as I should your buttocks
with cheap unmentionable toys
furthermore still, shall I consign such joy
to all the citizens of this hapless kingdom
what sophistry I gave you, and your broad-armed son
the fox could not build his own house
nor should I cut off the neck
of that which has its neck cut off

BEATITUDE THE SECOND

after five years, ten years had passed
such is the bane of any hand
aboard the Arghh-o-not who once sheared sheep
and for each prize, that crew, whose dreams
are with me nightly, biting their fingers
for more action, I'd swear I was the devil
at 3 o'clock this afternoon, almost at a panic
running another ship into harbor
though less than a minute before it hit land
to save their own worthless lives (and I was hunting
for more) a terrific sea blew up, lifting the deck
from its supports, tossing the women & children overboard
O listen to that mellisonant choir my dear Sesame
ra-hoor-khui-ker-plish, hoor-paar-kraat-ker-plosh
even Neptune's trident would fare badly

if paired with such tearful outpouring
mine is the mixture of sweet aquifers
giver of wave to ocean
begetter of huge serpents
bringer of calm to my beloved's eyes
the kteis, the eleytheria, the sarx
every abjurement, every Æon
a task that, from the first day, never ends
but wantonly in the backyard of all humankind
ghosted by these underwordly depths
where the ox plows its onion patch
and where I will have hold of your halter yet

BEATITUDE THE THIRD

eager to expand my conquest
and heap skeleton piles atop glebe & furrow
there upon the megalopolis I slept, dreaming of food
lowly concoctions, a trench of leeks
in a colossal pot, the date palm chopped & chewed
ground cassia bark & thyme
snake skin, turtle shell, milk & carnelian oil
seven times seven the heavenly heads
ten times ten the opulent horns
smitten smutten smoten schmutzen
sweetly tumble the churn to a boil
for I am no tutelary deity
who has pity for the man of one shekel
nor in the case of the scarlet wife
twice by the mattock, once by the hoe
then with the cita mace or the mitum mace
and a claw hammer to pulverize them both
O how my blood thickens like butter
come sit, my dear Ištar, at table with me
your throne-dais grows cold
yet no less world-wise
whose long beard casts a terrible eye
and over every scrap of earth
I tell you this, hinged on my one obsession
destruction has been given to me as to a dragon
who no longer fritters in the mêlée of battle
and because I have such perfect love of corn

BEATITUDE THE NINTH

even Lucifer's shadow trembles when I breathe
but who can vouch for that unpronounceable sky dweller
whom I revile far more
though given that neither have the stomach
for my filthiest loathing
I'll lavish my most diabolical acts

on that prosthetic-for-a-brain, man!
what mortal shall I bring to you first, my Diadem
to whom shall I truss the wings of this ill wind
which voice will prove loudest
put to fire, winnowed by pitchforks, laid on sticks
let the shepherd who declares his stock pure
have congress with all his sheep
then mummify only his flaccid form
so fate may pay homage to his immeasurable grief
let the temple scribe whose vainglorious lies
are told & retold, give quarry
to the bard's knife, ripping out his entrails
monstrous with snail & succubae
let the servant who takes up the plow
for his master's keep, find the gift
of my glittering hatchet on bended knee
O Messenger of Uggi, The Owl, the hour nears
send your blinding eye into the ground, gather up
the roots of your Great Tree, loose terrible menses
upon this world, summon the wild ram to its steppe
give no city quarter, belly to hot belly, as we have laid

BEATITUDE THE PURLOINED

FORSOOTH in the land of Ur-Bloodbath
every wretched derangement, every gangrenous
yawp, every unconscionable, low-down
bootlicking & busted-dream yowl
appeared as a single sound filling the sky, the bough
the cup, the staff, the staff with the cup, the burly
bough, a burl of burgeoning ocean, two burls
of she-goats, three burls of magnetic bees
four burling gazelles of burling white teeth
nine burly empresses of untold burl
their crimson fetlocks sheathed in stygian
fishnets trolloping south to east, then due east
with arms akimbo, dragging the torso
of man, putrefied of seed, boiled at the crossroads
his unburly loins purloined six cubits
below the canebrake, a basket of underpants
of bad quality in the reeds, O how the good morning
tasted, piece by piece, chucking the slag
that woeful perfume of poached flesh
neither eaten by impious fishes nor by crocodiles
but sleuthed, slogged, schlepped & sluiced
by the House of Elder Waters, it is I, APSU!
Loyal Troth of Ūsat, Ever Faithful Lover of Ēsi!
and for those more than mortal, and who have doubt
stand and be transmogrified! let no hesitation
come between blows! for I am returned, who was
once betrayed, to reclaim the Great Tamarisk!

GOING BACK TO WATER

having attended all the schools of serendipity

having thoroughly unlearned the alphabet
until I became perfectly legible

having camouflaged the silvery parts of my brain
with indistinguishable tears

having always understood other peoples' hopes
until they suicide my own

having fallen from a skyless sky only to find it was
never big enough
that I might flap my wings

having nearly drowned in my search
for the wreckage of the drunken boat

having taken refuge in the poisonous cave
of the cosmic eel

having come to blows with every invisible thing
that was trying to kill me

having emerged from that half-submerged Atlantis

having found a religion more powerful than god
in the eyes of a giant squid

having known no lexicon that contains the word
for my current predicament

CONCERTO IN NINE FRAGMENTS, ANDANTE

of all the thoughts I thought were my own

of all the years I've memorized myself to sleep

of all the places in my head that neither walk
nor dream in human form

of all the paths of inchworms & the unending
line of their kind

of all the holes dug in the mud and the seashells
crawled into & out of

of all the lights & burning skies that leave behind
the impression of a wish

of all the lips & pairs of lips that forgot to close
and open in precisely the right moment

of all the moments whose hands aren't ever sure
what they should do

of all the haloes circling earth in fear of what we
might do to each other next

WHAT IT'S ALL ABOUT

for Joe Brainard

looking down at my naked legs
even in sleep
I couldn't very well say
anything but yes
there were eight cherries
on a white oval dish
propped up
by a knee I have lived with
for years
outside in the sun
except for the great tan
and chaise longue
I was the only person I knew well
my days came unbuttoned
to the waist
studded with pink roses
sipping on Campari & sodas
orange flashes of green
I wanted to look like James Dean
but being left-handed as I am
and like the man
who remembers everything
sometimes I gathered my forces
so I could see better
it's like walking up the stairs
s
i
d
e
w b
a
c y
k s
w
a
r
d s l o w l y
s
the door opens
into a purple-lined box
as your life takes on a more
rectangular rhythm
but of course you win

INTERSTICITY

I was twelve in the third grade
she had beautiful hair
I was in love with her
playing the banjo
junkyard palace
magic consonants
a remarkable exuberance happened
I'd know those footprints anywhere
intersticity
yes it was good for me
within my limbs of all-knowledge
Lorca was another convention
there were great lullabies
a kind of dry flat stone
wonderfully acetate
always a superstition
I resent the ghettoing of disbelief
of dying in my dreams
luckily one of the workers who was
only mildly American
and from the point of hanging out
living with my father
that was a real education
his face shrunken and kind of in his lap
spaced on stuff like gladiators vs. the lions
he's got a special cigarette in one hand
it's like he was seeing X-Mas close up
from somewhere real far away
this was the music that really happened to me
all these genius kids looking like voodoo dolls
I wanted to slake my musical thirst
with something formal like "there were clouds
in my coffee, clouds in my coffee"
on so many levels part of me still
has to say blue sun

IN TRUTH MY NATURE WAS NEVER HALF-HUMAN

like watching snow fall from several
thousand feet
I didn't figure thus
artichokes and hearts of palm
licked my plate
I wish I could say
it was a bad vampire
because drinking blood
isn't vegetarian
but it wasn't
how should I feel about this?
well it reminds me of that trip to Alaska

I never took
that constant sense of driving
double-blind through the universe
connecting all the erratum
until everyone not even time existed
nowadays what happens
has happened for years
I've become the same age my ancestors
were when they were my age
sometimes I see their
eyes from the step bridge
in City Park lagoon
plumes of bliss pile up in my smoky brain
how many seconds go by
then everything starts to disappear

SLEEPING THE PIANO

I never dream to remember
it's always my love that I lunch
but will it stand under Simon's vigorous cross examination
Bernadette's good French badly translated
Niyi singing the audience along with African *amens*
and where will our wine live next?
yes I've finally made something for myself
and poured it into a glass
with some ice cubes and cut lemon
it's like that lovely girl who slept through
the entire poetry reading curled
up beside the piano
maybe all nights should begin
with Nina Simone or Ninette's voice
saying *the sun dips golden somewhere*
later at Molly's I watched birds fly
out the back of Andrei's head
they tattooed poems all over our bodies
we bought another round
raised a cheer & toasted all the gods
that rule from the clouds "O New Orleans
you float like the stairs of no heaven!"
next morning we pulled our stools
back up to the bar
and took turns dipping our hands
into a bucket of oysters
I wasn't sure whether we were saying hello or goodbye
it was barely sunny that day
the flowers were still flowering
but it was all figured in the eyes
a sufficient quantity of blue

WALKING THE LEVEE

raison d'être is a promise to keep scratching your head
mine feels like a drive-in movie
where all the missing parts of the universe
have melted onto the screen
O modern Thebes, what have you done with me
in one ear a spider spins its web of eyes
from my other comes the sound
of a confused butterfly
leaving the skin of its cocoon
does the sky ever pass through your bedroom?
it's not a question you can answer biblically
but if you've traveled far enough
up or down this earth
you've seen rivers flowing backwards
and known others
where one struck match
melts water into flame
Peace River a little east of Dawson Creek is like that
today I'll pretend it's the Mississippi
I'm walking the levee
lining up clouds over the tops of skyscrapers
I suppose the view is similar from the cemetery too
but that's a space where nothing talks
little roses, the black majestic ones
and if you're wondering what's burning
it's a small child
whose fever has become you

THE THEORY OF ANYTHING

I'm feeling a little less apocalyptic
the toilet seat isn't broken
Mina's toys are all over the floor
Megan's body is working
on the second unborn
occasionally a raccoon
passes through the front yard
yesterday I discovered
I could count birds in a tree
near the kitchen window
and peel shrimp at the same time
yeah it's true I'll probably never
find the emerald city or the tornado
that stole me from home
but then again my angels don't glare back at me
as much as they used to
and nowadays when the grim reaper
shows up shining his tiny flashlight
around in the back of my head
we both stop what we're doing
pour each other a double on the rocks
and instead of the usual
knock down drag out heart-to-heart
we just talk

THE NEREIDS OF SHALOM

The Nereids of Shalom is a hard luck tale of Chilean wine
stomped and crushed by the feet of a beautiful Guavian
princess who only knew sadness & the night of day

so she took to her own dervish shapes cut out of tissue
paper and drew circles where her forehead once grew
soon everyone wondered whether she could bake

the exquisite dessert where was the pan who could
how the butter now the cow and so it was in the land
of shimmering hands I appeared to hold her hand

but the *oră pentru tinutul de mana* was nigh and lo thus
by the remnants of quilts which kept no one warm
who knew the why the breath of sad the clouds

the junipers the sunflowers the reasons for knowing only
one more sea overgrown like eyelids like waterfalls why
each night the day was shut inside the skin of a tree

MY HUNGER HAS NO INDECISION

for Simon Pettet

my hunger has no indecision
about who's sitting at the table during dinner
if it's a rabbit not a turtle
nor a shank of cow
I imagine little whiskers twitching
inside your mouth
if it's a more unintelligible food
like couchon de lait
I bow my head accordingly
to the sadness the joy
which our hands doth make
if it's something pungent like sweetbreads
or slivers of olived liver
my nose becomes a long knife
and keeps us in stitches
if the feast comes with a specially prepared sauce
garnished with capers
I remove the capers
and pretend my life is complicated
like the specially prepared sauce

A *STUYVESANT BEE* &c

by Mike Topp

STATUS: I had a lot of trouble falling off a log.

[--------------------SPLASH---------------------]
Walk with your top hat upside down to improve your posture—a tip.

WORTHLESS COUPONS

....

|

....

|

....

|

....

STRAY DIALOG:

Customer : Hi there, I need a toilet plunger.

Employee : No.

{}

SOME COMPLAINTS OF ORDINARY CITIZENS

•Don't have billions in offshore account.

•Didn't recently pick out 13th wife at annual virgin festival.

•No private army and air force.

THUMBPRINTS

- -

|
|
|
|

- -

BONNIE AND CLYDE HISTORICAL FICTION

At 7:00 a.m., two detectives, Sherlock Holmes and Nero Wolfe, were at 2030 Henry Hudson Parkway in Riverdale, a white brick twenty-five story monstrosity overlooking the river with a primordial view of the Jersey Palisades. It was not Clyde Barrow's current address; that would be a five-room crash pad in Cobble Hill, an *Our Gang* pot-stanky garden apartment in which none of his just-woken roomies could even tell the detectives where Clyde originally hailed from. Riverdale was the address on his driver's license, also home to a Bonnie Parker, presumably Clyde's girlfriend or at least a blood relation. Clyde was texting her now. His breath smelled like pigeon—*STOOL PIGEON!!* •

SCENIC VIEW REST AREA

---A THOUSAND WORDS---

Went to the dentist today and spoke to the receptionist about my missing necklace. She said she'd ask. √

DIVINE LOVE: God rains his love down on us every day. But we don't feel that love, because our ego is like a giant umbrella that we hold over our heads. What we need to do is put that umbrella away in the ego's umbrella stand—then we will feel God's love. Ego's umbrella stand, in black walnut or mahogany. $7,500.

GROUNDHOG DAY

Well, gang, it's just ONE MONTH until Groundhog Day—so for this tim around I recommend the following:

-OVERSIZED DESIGNER SUNGLASSES
-PUNXSUTAWNEY PHIL CANNED VEGETABLES
-BEER MUGS (Just one)
-GRADE A EGGS A LA KING
-FOAM TOP HAT
-EMOTICONS :(

QUICK FACT

Between the ages of 14 and 17 I saw "Enter the Dragon" 22 times before I stopped counting.

RESURRECTION

Even though my brain is being dissolved by salt my urine is made of diamonds.

MADAME BOVARY

The Person I am most interested in is Madame Bovary. At the same time, I'm afraid to read anything by the French lady.

SASQUATCH STORIES

Donna stretched out a hand and caught hold of the edge of the coat and tugged at it; he pulled up the window and turned. He bent and put his hands on the fur over her breasts and kissed her hard on the lips.

THE PET STORE

A very sad thing happened at the pet store. Debbie, Steve's mother, became very sick and died.

A WILD RUMOR

Paul Bunyon has a spice rack.

OUR MAN IN MANHATTAN

As Kirby Olson noted back in *Cyber Corpse #8*:

"Topp's work is conceptual and revolutionary and requires an understanding of the Fluxus sensibility (http://www.fluxus.org) which enlivened the art world and Peace Movement of the 1960s… What Yoko Ono and the other artists of Fluxus were doing was to take the sting out of the judgmental territorializations of art in order to 'draw out the revolutionary power of the order-word; for the question was not how to elude the order-word but how to elude the death-sentence it envelops, how to develop its power of escape'" (Deleuze 110).

Meaning there are colossal philosophies within Topps' mucho economy-sized epics. Sometimes they impersonate haikus; other times they're disguised as two or three whacky phrases performing stand-up comedy—but ultimately, like microbacteria, their often deceiving simplicities contain multitudes of finite squiggle-hairs that are Rococo with luminous colors and textured depths reaching beyond the eye of the microscope. Just take this mind-warper, for example:

FRANKLY:
A rose is a rose is a -------<@.

And that's the way it is (ms).

FROM *BRAINS: A ZOMOIR*

by Robin Becker

Lucy and I were hiding in the basement. We were with the boxes of Christmas decorations—no Chanukah junk, mind you, no menorah, nothing Hebrew in sight—and the never-used tent and Lucy's treadmill, also never used. Our life's detritus was all around us and my cheek was on the concrete and Lucy's hand was in my hair. The bite on my shoulder throbbed like a hard-on and I closed my eyes and I died.

Let that sink in: I died.

There was a moment of suspension when I was no longer human and not yet zombie. My body was nothing, was as good as a couch cushion or a blow-up doll or the giant plastic Santa mocking us in the corner. Walt Disney cryogenically frozen. Pinocchio before the breath of life, hanging limp from his strings.

It's true what they say about viewing your corpse from above. I floated near the ceiling, gazing at Lucy and what used to be me, and in that instant, I was as content as one of the Lord's sheep, a member of His flock. The zombie horde seemed far away; I could barely hear them pounding at the cellar door. My ears were flooded with celestial music, the music of the spheres. It sounded like twee Brit pop. Was it angels with harps? Maybe. Belle & Sebastian? Perhaps. Was it Jesus strumming an acoustic guitar like some traveling barefoot hippie? In my dreams.

Because let's rationalize: The whole "near-death experience," the whole light-at-the-end-of-the-tunnel trip, is a trick of the brain, a hallucination. It is not a supernatural event, but one last fantasy brought to you by your endorphins to mitigate the absolute terror of death. To inspire hope against the nothingness we all fear. The whole cessation of ego and self-hood business. The loss of the world. Because everyone wants to exist, don't they? But we all die in the end.

Unless we're undead.

Then there are the suicides. Hanging themselves on reinforced beams in their empty Seattle apartments; overdosing on pills in the bedrooms of their mothers; blowing their brains out with rifles or shotguns or pistols; starting cars in garages and reading Dostoevsky until sleep; driving mini-vans off cliffs with children strapped in the backseat. They screw existence. In the ass.

Bear in mind, this is a zombie talking—a supernatural being. What do I know? I might not even be real.

Oh, ontology.

Regardless of religion or science, there I was, floating near the ceiling and at peace, when the girly music of the spheres turned into Norwegian death metal and I was ripped away from the fuzzy blankets of cloudland and confronted with demons and devils and a descent into hell. I was whisked into some sort of meat tube, like a large intestine, where trapped souls screamed at me from polyp walls and everything was flaming orange and too hot. Munch's *The Scream* was there, the painted man's hand on the side of his face. A child tattooed with the mark of the beast turned into a stampede of wild horses running away from a Gothic mansion which morphed into a fat lady in pearls laughing. The typical horror movie shtick. Cliché, but true.

Then I was reborn.

Let that sink in.

Yea, though I walk through the shadow of the valley of death, I fear no evil. For I am evil. And I am the shadow. And I am death.

Not just zombie but archetype. Not just villain but hero. Jungian shadow, id and ego. Man is woman. Ovaries are testes. Cats are dogs.

There's Michael and Laurie, Leatherface and Sally, Leatherface and Stretch, Norman and Marion. Need I go on?

I opened my eyes. Lucy screamed. The zombie horde broke through the door and I lunged, lunged, lunged at my wife and she was lunch.

Heavens she was tasty. We ate her communally: the fresh-faced blonde zombette from next door; the nuclear family from across the street, which, as a result of decay, truly did have 2.5 kids; the haggard waitress zombie from Denny's, varicose veins now black and inky; the suspicious loner zombie who never gave out Halloween candy; the teenage geek zombie with his pimples and Lord of the Rings t-shirt; and me, the professor zombie, with my tortoise shell glasses and robin's egg blue shirt.

This was no symbolic eating, no representational wafer. We didn't just break bread—we broke flesh; we drank blood. It was a living Eucharist.

Lucy's still in me now. Transubstantiation. Her remains remain. Forever and ever. Amen.

Burp.

ROD'S LONELY NIGHT

by Aram Saroyan

In the winter of 1976 I committed the professional and personal faux pas of giving a poetry reading with Rod McKuen. It took place at the Veterans Auditorium in downtown San Francisco and was supposed to be a benefit for the San Francisco State University poetry program. Lewis MacAdams, my friend and fellow resident of Bolinas, the radical seacoast town at the western edge of Marin County, was just then employed as director of the program. I had wanted a reading in that year's series, of course, but Lewis and I were poetry competitors as well as friends. I should say that poets, generally perceived as ivory tower dreamers and underpaid to the point of extinction, are among the most vainglorious and unforgiving in the matter of readings, appointments, anthologies, and the like, none of it amounting to a hill of beans. In the months prior to the McKuen/Saroyan slate being set my suspicion was that Lewis wasn't going to include me on his schedule of readers, and this despite all the stuff I'd written recently, including full page poems in *Rolling Stone, New Age, The Village Voice,* and the *New York Times Sunday Magazine*.

Is it any wonder I was copiously engaged at that moment trying to switch into more welcoming genres, from book reviews and magazine articles to a novel and a biography? *Rolling Stone* had printed the first of my full page poems, "Lines for My Autobiography," several years before, and I had built on a relationship with the magazine, specifically with its editor-in-chief, Jann Wenner, to aid me in discovering a path into the open air of modern America, so to speak, and out of the tiny, vituperative sandbox of American poetry. In that ill-appointed domain you had the fortunate few sitting on little perches--castles in the sand indeed—and, otherwise, endless lunatics with pails and shovels, erupting water and sand fights, booze, blood, piss and mucous, carrying on 24/7, bitching, yelling, punching each other, crying, marrying their students, bragging, getting knocked unconscious by their younger wives, and soiling themselves. Did I leave anything out? This is simply the American literary life, sub-genus Poets. Gregory Corso, an outlander, said it beautifully, I think: Poetry is great; it's the poets who fuck it up.

One of the ideas I got for *Rolling Stone* was that I should interview Rod McKuen, at the time the world's best selling poet as well as a singer songwriter recently celebrated for his hit song "Jean" from the film *The Prime of Miss Jean Brodie*. McKuen seemed to me an interesting subject for a number of reasons, which I ran by Wenner over the phone, as I remember. That McKuen was enormously popular and also versatile was a given. At the same time, his poetry was dismissed—by most of my friends, for instance, so that it constituted a little postural shift for me to sign on as the interviewer, in effect giving McKuen what he obviously needed not in the least, the imprimatur of a younger poet's attention. Still, he was strictly from the wrong side of the tracks. If he'd been to Iowa City, the home of the famous University of Iowa's Writers Workshop, it was probably for a cocktail lounge one-nighter on a long-forgotten record tour. On the heels of my second book of minimal poetry with Random House, I had passed through myself and visited my friends Ted Berrigan and Anselm Hollo, and spoken to the students in their classes, but been unceremoniously denied a poetry reading by George Starbuck, who told me sheepishly that he wasn't sure he liked minimal poetry. As much as I could applaud this soul-searching on his part, I thought he might have given me a chance to argue my case.

McKuen's work was plain-spoken, romantic, and of course completely out of the academic loop. There's a species I think of these days as poetry church mice, perennially going their appointed rounds on campuses all across America, where

I knew myself not to be welcome, either. On glancing into McKuen's books, I felt that while he didn't personally mesmerize me in the way he did the millions who were his fans, he was just as good or better than dozens of these others. Here was a guy, after all, who started writing things down when he was a second-bill folk singer with little hope of receiving any literary reception whatsoever. And several million copies of his books later, he was seemingly a bigger pariah than he had been at the start. That interested me. He wrote sincerely out of his own need, and that wasn't the worst reason to pick up a pen. That he captured the attention of so many people testified to something, I thought, that made the matter larger than adolescent lovelorn jottings, if in fact that is what they were, and perhaps comprised a kind of window on the national psyche.

Wenner, a quick study, holds the issues of his magazine in mind like a super computer. I once had the sensation that he was doing a quick "search engine" review of his universe in front of my eyes as I sat opposite him at a table in his office one afternoon decades before the Internet, and that his brain worked a good deal better than mine, at least at this appointed task.

Wenner said okay. Rod and I did an interview. Annie Liebovitz came to his Beverly Hills house with me to take photographs, and we spent the night there, me in "the room with the ghost," Rod told me. I woke up in the middle of the night, and sure enough, there it was—ectoplasmic but clearly impalpable and harmless, at the foot of the bed. Annie photographed Rod, and me too. Maybe they would run a picture of the two of us on the cover of *Rolling Stone*?

Then there were delays, and other problems which have fallen away with time, and for some reason the interview never appeared. In the meantime, though, I had an ace in the hole with Lewis. Would he give me a place in his line up with Rod McKuen on board? Do it as a fund raiser? My own venality rises, if the gentle reader hasn't already detected it.

Poor Rod, who was then in his early forties, the late beneficiary of a huge American-style success, but in his bones a Western-style lonesome traveler, someone who'd never known his actual father and knocked around from one end of town to the other, from night clubs to the rodeo, picking up bits and pieces everywhere before he self-published *Stanyon Street and Other Sorrows* and sold thousands of copies out of the back of his car after his singing engagements.

He was, as Annie Liebovitz immediately noticed, extremely savvy in front of the camera, while I was clearly a novice. ("Aram," she told me, "don't smile.") At the same time, Rod had a kind of disarming home-grown ease in conversation that didn't actually go very far. Not a devoted reader of contemporary poetry, he was an aficionado of song stylists from Jeri Southern to Frank Sinatra, for whom he'd recently written an album. Having lost his voice during a marathon tour for a minor hit during the fifties, he had parlayed the permanent damage into a pleasing sandpaper vocal signature. *Rolling Stone* interested him, of course, because it was an unlikely venue, and a big one, and he availed himself of me and Annie in a spirit of animated, but, one couldn't help but feel, guarded engagement.

* * *

As I envisioned it, the reading would reintroduce Rod with an official imprimatur to the town he had celebrated in his first hit book (Stanyon Street is in the Haight-Ashbery district). In retrospect, the mistake was to promote the reading instead of simply promoting an appearance by Rod McKuen. With a miniscule budget, it was hard for San Francisco State to ante up for even a small ad in *The San Francisco Chronicle,* and so we rather heedlessly relied on the free publicity available through the local radio and television stations, with me along for the ride. It was wrong to go this route because

McKuen's legion fans weren't interested in poetry per se, but in Rod, period. As word circulated about the reading, with my association and San Francisco State's a part of the package, my guess is that 99 percent of Rod's fans decided to give it a pass.

With an auditorium that could hold a thousand or more, we had something over 100 people, a large percentage of them poets, including Michael McClure and Edward Dorn, as well as the local press. Lewis introduced me and then Rod in turn, we each read, and there was a brief question period at the end, but it was clear from the turnout that something had gone wrong. Julie Smith, the reporter for *The Chronicle* who went on to write detective novels, wrote a piece for the morning paper titled "Rod's Lonely Night." After the reading I'd talked briefly with her and got the sense that she was going to go after Rod, but then she really wasn't the right reporter for the assignment. The story that night was one she didn't acknowledge, and probably wasn't aware of: at least two major American poets had come to see and hear Rod, and it would have been interesting to hear the commentary of McClure and Dorn, as well as the young Andrei Codrescu, among others.

Not long afterwards, Rod came to town again for a week-long engagement at the Fairmont Hotel, which also wasn't well received by *The Chronicle.* The day after the opening, with the review in the paper, he was unreachable, which to a youngster like myself was incomprehensible. Now I understand perfectly well. He was exhausted. A poet-singer-songwriter who had been trashed twice in a town he had celebrated, he had a show to do that night and was running on empty. Rod did the show, and after a week of them, went on to someplace else. He was, of course, a consummate pro. Wherever he is—I think he still lives in Beverly Hills, though he keeps a low profile these days—I wish him well, and apologize.

SUDDENLY

by Jim Gustafson

for Roy Castleberry

Suddenly I was no longer petrified
of being lucid. Suddenly being wet
and hungry and a thousand miles
from home held no further surprises.
Suddenly the summer swooped down
like a raven unto a big juicy hambone.
Suddenly it was winter again, and
there we were with a half-gallon of
frozen cactus juice. Suddenly the
Blue Absolutely granted us a reprieve.
Suddenly, without even a warning
grunt, the wounded warthog of real
life lowered its head and charged.
Suddenly you were stricken with tusk
luck. Suddenly sensation swelled and
the white room hushed. Suddenly
enlightened bloat seemed adequate
but we kept looking for something to
compare it with anyway. Suddenly
the Curse of Immediate Gratification
lifted. Suddenly you were granted
your exit visa and could leave for Big
Lights Bright City but didn't
want to. Suddenly being an American
in America seemed like a pretty
good idea. Suddenly everyone latched
on to your philosophy of never
doing the same dance step twice and
you were hailed as a great liberator.
Suddenly the procession took a sharp
right into the private courtyard
of the Clown King and all Hell broke
loose. Suddenly surrender seemed
so perfunctory as to be ludicrous and
surviving so real as to be surreal.
Suddenly there was another sham-o-
rama mythology wrapped in synthetic
pathos and held together by dung-
flavored gum that needed to be
debunked. Suddenly Lotto Mentality
nosed out Work Ethic on the
backstretch of the decade and the
tote board lit up and everybody who
won gathered up their filthy lucre and
got out of your way. Suddenly the
elevator stopped between the 20th and
21st centuries. Suddenly we counted
ourselves among the unvanquished.
Suddenly lives without middles
merged in miracles. Suddenly the
thrill was back, stronger than ever.

FIRMER TOFU POETRY

by Joel Dailey

4 THINGS ALL GUYS KEEP PRIVATE

for Lucille Ball

I keep reminding myself   just about anybody would

3 times the power of ordinary fish oil

Memo to self   hotdog all the way tomorrow & tomorrow

& tomorrow

Oof

Do you (yes you do don't you) have a visual

My portfolio lost in a multi-cat household

Outside of which a white Chrysler with front end damage

waits

*

Incumbent upon me

*

1. Oscar de la Hoya

2. the uppercut

3. the doppler effect

4. the abundance of Ouch

30 THINGS TO PUT YOU IN A GOOD MOOD

for Moose Skowron

Relationship experts in flipflops

Riffraff uptick

An unstable environment attracts unstable personalities

Subject inhales spaghetti

Never take a bribe from a guy nicknamed "Pampy"

There is always more leeway

Be aware that I am a frolicsome person who cherish concealed

    & furtive quickie

Extra lift   plus maximum separation

Subject recalls toast   fondly

Anybody with any brains already left the bowl

Specifically designed, I was tooling down Dopefiend Street

    when it hit me

HI MOTOR MOUTH

There you were   tripodinal

Maybe the whole time

The way of the narrative

Uppity

Yearning to be

To the exclusion of all else

A doorbell

& who strides in

Baseball Hall of Famer Brooks Robinson is 70 today

MY PLEASURE

    for Goose Gossage

Here I sit at the open window

  dirty screen

Breeze out of the southeast

Wondering

If the avant-garde is passing me by

THE EAR WAX REMOVAL SYSTEM

for Larry Storch

Here we are once again

My upturned doorknobs

Attempting to resist intention

But first I must commit personal hygiene

I've gone from Facebook to Assbook

You see   it's my leg

I used to be muy telegenic

But now I phone it in

Nimble   fresh mind   firmer tofu

I've purchased the Ear Wax Removal System

So I'd be sure to hear the Muse

Whispering along the keyboard to Mal Waldron

My own claim to Immortality

This flaccid   overwritten   beerbarrel polka

I'm trying to hit one outta here

While maintaining the fluid lines of the Interior

At variance   rundownbankrupt

The tv promises sudden relief

Avoid the dog

Don't fluctuate

You scratch my back I'll scratch my ass

TIRE KINGDOM AUDIBLE

Mister Windshield

The earflaps are detachable so shutup.org

My demons rebound anxiety off the blue backboard of my brain

Be American

Take, in fact, a pill

Or "I'm gonna start collecting me a few scalps"

#1 tough guys in shorts

The previous owner may be previously disturbed

& transformed by water molecules

Now it's the waiting mode in the waiting room   tv nose

You begin to answer your own questions

Know what I mean   Yessir

What's tossed from a speeding car Dirty sexy sex

Who's spanking who   The feduciary

A bunch of overall-wearing farmers somehow got hold of a tractor

          beam   UPS delivery mixup?

Just let me say my position on this issue has always been decidedly

          pro-farmer   I adore corn

          Why   some of my best friends are farmers

          Don't taze me, bro, don't taze me

          From Ho-Hum to Hot   twilight spreading sky pink

          I am forced to live like gypsy

          You have reached the desk of Brett Evans

          Nodding off into Dreamland now   (& then)

          All the little stories in my head

"You got the Camry?"

WHAT'S WRONG WITH LOU DOBBS? Or, FEEL MORE AT HOME IN THE ISLANDS WITH INSTANT HAWAIIAN

You've earned an exciting new cell phone

Just ahead of the opening bell

Crawfish   fascinating wildlife   in a ditch

Now & then we wrestle with indoor air quality issues

"It's just like being inside but you're outside"

Somedays Existence is a huge challenge or you've spawned

          a designated parking spot

Connectivity has been frequently established   but lost

For instance, "drug mule" as in "You're a fucking drug mule.

          aren't you, Carl?"

Subarctic adventures abound

Impulse items thrive

A team of Specialists flies in & departs the next morning,

          rusty fishhooks in their mouths

"Gee, Mister D, what did Poetry ever do to you that you would

          denigrate it so?"

Early on it was girl on girl

Now it's ape on cantaloupe

The imaginary line is drawn in the real sandbox by a lopped off

          thumb.

Ladies & G's, the next generation of foam

AMERICA'S LAUNDROMAT

by Mike Topp

The other day I was walking around and saw a place called "America's Laundromat." I thought it would be much bigger.

WHAT MAKES AMERICA GREAT THE WORK OF JOE BRAINARD

The Nancy Book, by Joe Brainard
Los Angeles, Siglio Press, 2008

If... by Joe Brainard
Los Angeles, Siglio Press, 2008
www.sigliopress.com

Joe Brainard was both a great artist and a great writer, a *rara avis*, in the best of times. His epic *I Remember*, is one of the literary accomplishments of the late 20th century, a long poem in which every line begins with the words "I remember," and then goes on to recall everything that Joe Brainard's memory was able to recall, from his earliest childhood to the moment of writing. The swift and witty practice of memory in *I Remember* is an exercise in truth and accuracy, a manual of American culture, pop and not, and a psychoanalytical tour-de-force directed not just at specific and personal neuroses, but at the incurable and painfully amusing maladies of a whole society. Joe Brainard, like his New York School friends and contemporaries—Kenward Elmslie, John Ashbery, Bill Berkson, Ron Padgett, and Ted Berrigan among them—managed to ride with verve the zeitgeist of an age rich in creative stimulation and ready-made for revolution. Joe was a Pop artist, in the sense that his art, like his writing, blew out the frames of genre and the conventions of the medium, and partook with pleasure and energy from the demotic. *The Nancy Book* chronicles the adventures of the comic-book character Nancy in Joe's own world, in collaboration with Bill Berkson, Ted Berrigan, Robert Creeley, Frank Lima, Frank O'Hara, Ron Padgett and James Schuyler. This beautifully produced edition comes with essays by Ann Lauterbach and Ron Padgett. *If...* is a series of postcards presenting Nancy in a variety of "if" situations. The reprinting of these extremely rare works by Joe Brainard is an event for at least two reasons: 1. *The Nancy Book* is a masterwork of collaboration from the age of collaboration between artists and writers, a practice of instantly communicable delight that occured only twice in the 20th century: the Dada-Surrealist age, 1915-1935, and the New York School, 1957-1973, and 2. while comix have become "acceptable" for both "high" art and commercial translation (into movies), they have never attained the freshness and impertinence of being recast for the first time with such vigurous insouciance. Joe Brainard was a genius who had the good luck of living at the right time and having genius friends. Snap up these books, people, you never know when another epoch of public misery and artistic glory will sweep us away. When it does, you'll have guides (ac).

ASSORTED SYLLABRIES

by Skip Fox

TITLE IN BOLD

mind in hold of language, that which casts *us* like dice across time, abyss of page, or room's silence, and which throws us as well into each other with such fury, with instruments also the product of language as we are in a history of words, ancient hatreds singing "Least we never get even" into the street, across mountains and desert, but also cast over stone as a stream glistens, yet would we cross, even to the ankles and knees, would we find the next stone we were sure between each but the current gets suddenly swift and the weather changes the mountains darken and we are caught out in a rush of water up our legs falls certain screaming in mind's dark ear, from slightest slip of phrase to tragedy of sentence in one swift . . . as though we found it there, and as sure.

LATE SUMMER

Crowds of clouds each day, thunderstorms every afternoon. Deepening sounds down season's halls resonate in dream. Last night my son tried to stab me in my sleep. Or a man stands on a plateau where small, fat animals are dying. In his mind there was too much of what the intelligence community would call chatter for him to discern any patterns of movement, groupings, messages of mal intent, or sudden losses from stores he thought secure. Lightning in the bowels, black sky tinged with green. Thunder rolls beneath summer's walls, brows at 20,000 feet. Lawn still growing as hair on skull unaware the grand engine has come to a halt and now reverses itself. This time forever. Your last refuge is being torn asunder, nowhere to return, even if you *could* remember.

NIRVANA

libretto of crickets and cars before dawn, Jeri is playing monkey, tearing the house a new one, markets hover on the borders of consciousness full of friendly people wearing wooden shoes and hats, they would fill your pipe, baskets of music and fruit hang with fronds from the rafters, and air drifts slowly down, with light, someone is playing a joke over the radio, a small group of old men are sharing coffee in what they know will be their last years, laughing, they are blessed, words come with their own illumination, like sharks and hands, hard tasking of the self even to the edge from which there is no return, & over which no grace descends but that one sets his life to the ripeness of experience, only Gaughin and few others, all islanders, saw it first as fresh paint.

PROEM from *Skin*

portal through which we are seen and whereby we see, as
indeed, hands have eyes in the dark and sight at each
extent of us, over all our every margin, unwrapped you
could fill a room with dust, canvas of sin, cheap costume
from props, that with which we wrap the creature (what's
crawling around just beneath, your mother?, past trapped
like hornet under shirt?), or map to ancient villages filled
with laughter, music and dances that will make you spill
your drink, the skin has its own climate, winters in its
south, where an amphitheater opens onto a harbor, sunset,
an old woman telling those gathered that her story will
scare them, then going about it slowly, deliberately, and
everybody on the last sentence jumping out of their skin.

EVEN WHEN

flap of bird's wing, silk wave laps shore then retreats in
suck of sound, soft inhalation, prolonged waiting, that is
we're only waiting . . . , would we ride the crest of moment's movement if we could?, we would do so gladly,
simple as that, logic as clear as what's *behind* the mirror
(or do I mean *beneath*?), maybe I mean the *concept* of
identity, moon as mirror of prose, both here and not, state
though it seems so worthy ignorance, the inanity of the
populus defined as the absence of all others, looking over its
shoulder, at whatever it is stands there, before us, someone's impending death, the house is on fire, or morning's
fog, dripping even as it gathers to resolve into a day as
yet another in the world which we ignore at our peril,
dissolution and the crude irreversibility of time.

SUFFERIN' SUCCOTASH

beets meatloaf plenty of Campbell's Soup *Reader's
Digest Time Life* television lawn snow watches bikes a
dog basketball long distance running Phyllis Platt's legs
& smile cars plays birdwatching making radios sweet
and sour pussy homework bored senseless in every class
the halls of junior high impressive after coming from the
suburbs of Detroit with their squat notions of a "physical
plant" and then in Bowling Green there were alleys & a
mind to explore them the pull of graffiti the slightly lost
lobotomized look of those born and raised in same place
they are currently living especially if that place is small
town America awash in drug stores and Christmas dis-
plays yet there are some nights dark & deep as any winter
where a man kills his wife or a child tortures a favorite pet.

GO TO…

a play by Bob May

CAST OF CHARACTERS

SON

FATHER

FOUR POLICEMEN

JUDGE

FRANK

WIFE

(AT RISE: FATHER and SON are discovered standing in front of two big, brightly painted doors. The right door has a big number one painted on it. The left door has a big number two painted on it. The SON holds a suitcase.)

SON
Goodbye father.

(They embrace. SON moves to door number one. At the door he stops and turns to his FATHER.)

SON (cont.)
Do you think it's a good choice?

FATHER
It's a choice.

SON
But is it a good choice?

FATHER
It's your choice. At least you have one. When I was your age I didn't have one. I was told what to do.

SON
Please tell me what to do.

FATHER
I can't. It's a new age you live in.

SON
Maybe I should choose this one?

(SON moves to door number two.)

FATHER
I wish I had the answer.

SON
No, I think my original choice was correct.

(He moves back to door number one.)

SON (cont.)
Please try to explain my choice to her.

(SON opens door number one and enters. FATHER exits. The door shuts and immediately red LIGHTS start flashing, sirens SOUND, the doors fly out, and SON is surrounded by four POLICEMEN.)

COP
You're under arrest.

SON
What did I do?

COP
You left your wife.

SON
But she was not being honest.

COP
Tell it to the judge.

(LIGHTS flash and SOUND is heard as the four POLICEMEN drag SON to a JUDGE, who sits behind a large desk.)

JUDGE
Guilty! You are sentenced to life in prison.

(JUDGE hits his gavel on the desk. Prison bars fly in. LIGHTS flash and SOUND is heard as the four POLICEMEN drag SON to a prison cell. They throw him in and then stand at the four corners of the cell. FRANK catches SON.)

SON
Thanks.

FRANK
Frank. Just call me Frank.

SON
Thanks Frank.

FRANK
What are ya in for?

SON
For making a choice.

FRANK
Me too. It was either him or me.

SON
Murder?

FRANK
Self defense.

SON
Would you do it again?
Now that you know the outcome?
I wish I could choose again.

COP
You ... son. You've been paroled!
Make better choices in the future.

(The cell bars fly out. FRANK and four POLICEMEN exit. The two doors fly in. LIGHTS flash and SOUND is heard as this shift takes place. FATHER enters and moves to SON.)

FATHER
Did you learn anything, son?

SON
Hindsight is great.

FATHER
You mean you'd make a different choice if you could do it over?

SON
To avoid prison ... yes.

(FATHER indicates door number two.)

FATHER
Luckily, you have a choice.

(They embrace. SON walks to door number two. He stops and turns to FATHER.)

SON
Do you think it's a good choice?

FATHER
It's a choice.

SON
But is it a good choice?

FATHER
It's your choice. At least you have one.
When I was your age I didn't have one.
I was told what to do.

SON
Please tell me what to do.

FATHER
I can't. It's a new age we live in.

SON
I hope things are different.

(SON opens door two. FATHER exits. The door shuts. The doors fly out. SOUND: Merry music. SON smiles. Then suddenly the LIGHTS begin to flash and SOUND is heard as a bed spins in with two people in it, laughing and enjoying one another post sex. The faces of the two in bed can't be seen.)

SON (cont.)
Nothing's changed, wife.
You're still not being honest with me.

(WIFE sits up. The man's face is still hidden.)

WIFE
I thought you left.

SON
I chose to come back.

WIFE
You never could commit to a choice.

(The man sits up in the bed. It is FRANK.)

SON
Frank? It was you? She was cheating with you?

(FRANK gets out of bed. He pulls a gun from under the pillow and points it at SON.)

FRANK
Self defense!

SON
Bullshit ... murder.

(SON and FRANK fight. The gun goes off. FRANK falls to the floor. Immediately red LIGHTS flash and sirens SOUND. The bed spins off, FRANK and WIFE exit, and the four POLICEMEN surround SON.)

COP
You're under arrest.

SON
It was self-defense.

COP
Tell it to the Judge.

(LIGHTS flash and SOUND is heard as the four POLICEMEN drag SON to a JUDGE, who sits behind a large desk.)

JUDGE
Guilty! You are sentenced to life in prison.

(JUDGE hits his gavel on the desk. Prison bars fly in. LIGHTS flash and SOUND is heard as the four POLICEMEN drag SON to a prison cell. They throw him in and then stand at the four corners of the cell. FRANK catches SON.)

FRANK
What are ya in for?

SON
For making a choice.

FRANK
Me too. Murder?

SON
Self defense.

FRANK
Would you do it again?

(The two men sit and stare at one another. LIGHTS fade to black.)

LOVE SCHOOL

by Richard Martin

Instead of making love to his wife Molly, T-Bone preferred listening to Sports Radio *650 WMOAN*. T-Bone had no idea how his intense commitment to listening to Sports Radio *650 WMOAN* had trumped his desire for a conjugal life with his steadfast and faithful wife, but he figured that it might be like many other things that had come about in his life as a T-Bone, i.e., there was no rational explanation for it – and despite the long haul through myth and superstition to the logos-light of mind and the enormous need for the human animal to be rational – there were still many things or phenomena that could not be explained by logic or a penchant for syllogism.

Take T-Bone's feet, for instance. According to him, they had definitely shrunk and perhaps were still shrinking without any rational cause or reason. Situated as he was in *The Decade of Small* (T-Bone had a knack—an annoying knack {issue to some}—of capturing and recapping his life as a series of named decades, such as *The Decade of Suck* or *The Decade of Gas*, which he then would turn loose on someone just entering that decade {say their thirties} regaling them with a laundry list of unfortunate things that had happened to him during said decade), his feet had shrunk from 9 ½ in size to 8 ½ in size. And, of course, there were other things shrinking too during *The Decade of Small* that T-Bone took note of, but, uncharacteristically, kept to himself.

Molly, his persistently patient wife, tried to tell and reassure him that his feet were, in fact, definitely not shrinking and that the illusion (delusion) that they were could be explained by understanding the proclivities of shoe manufacturers in a global market.

"T-Bone, honey," she said. "It simply has to do with different manufacturers setting different standards for the basic 9 ½ foot."

"Yeah, right, Lily," T-Bone said, "there's always a perfectly rational explanation for everything. God forbid, if it's not global markets, but rather global warming taking it to my feet!"

True enough, the ice sheets and glacial facial expressions of the Arctic were giving way to an increase in temperature, and for years—in what could only be labeled as a prescient warning—T-Bone had complained of hot toes, without actually considering (or realizing) that his toes (thus feet) were victims of a pernicious post-industrial technological paradigm which stoked the planet into an eerie and uncomfortable sweat (box).

"Oh, cut it out, T-Bone," Molly countered. A sneaker made by *Mizuno* in China might be a 10 in relation to your present notion of a 9 ½, while a dress pair of *Ecco's* from Denmark registers an 8 ½ in describing the present size of your feet."

"That makes a hell a lot of sense," T-Bone said, turning away from her into his morning paper.

But Molly persisted (after tinkling her bowl of Special K with her spoon—something that drove T-Bone to distraction {but not here, thank God}):

"Women have gone through size tricks and manipulations their entire lives without paying the slightest attention to it. Manufacturers understand that a woman who wears a size 9 dress and can suddenly fit into a size 5—without setting down a single donut—will be thrilled by her sudden improved look and even prompted to buy a few more accessories to go with her new outfit and look."

But T-Bone would have none of it. He rose above the morning paper like a red-faced moon stranded on a chunk of ice with a distraught polar bear.

"Bullshit!" he exclaimed. "My feet have shrunk! I can't help it you if you don't believe it."

It was during this *Decade of Small* that Sports Radio *650 WMOAN* began to fester in T-Bone's mind, knocking Molly and him from a loving and productive relationship in the sack. T-Bone caught the sports radio babble on his way to work and back from it each day, spending hours tuned to *650 MOAN* (re: the ennui of FM pop culture songs in his veins) while stuck in traffic and staring down others with road rage in their eyes. Although not much of an athlete (he quit baseball as a youngster after laboring on farm teams for years before finally making it to Little League in his last year of eligibility, only to be hit in the nuts on the first pitch, as the lead off batter for *Miller Dodge*, by a monster child hurling smoke from just thirty feet away), he grew fascinated with the travails and troubles of today's multimillion dollar athletes—relentlessly reported on and scrutinized by *MOAN*'s own Fatso and Motormouth (*the talent*) – as they (star athletes – not role models) were caught and filmed fighting in bars, cheating on wives, and driving fiery sports cars at exorbitant speeds in the dead of night. Along with stats—intricate and mind-numbing stats—on every aspect of the game—any game: baseball, football, hockey, basketball—with the appropriate drubbing and belittling for less manly sports (tennis, golf), and just the right dose of right-wing foot stomping: THE WAR IS GOOD; A WOMAN PRESIDENT WOULD BE BAD, REALLY BAD; IT'S NOT ABOUT RACE FOR US; Fatso and Motormouth knew what a *NATION OF MISERABLE MISCREANTS*, stuck in traffic, wanted to hear and which simultaneously kept them perched atop Number 1 in the ratings game.

When foreplay disappeared from the pre-game of sex like a major leaguer's inability to lay down a bunt, Molly grew alarmed that *The Decade of Small* (mindedness) might be getting out of hand, and after an all-consuming three-minute session with her man, she tried to address the subject.

"T, honey," she said. "What's wrong?"

"Huh," T-Bone said. "Wrong with what?"

"Our love-life, silly," Molly said.

"Oh, that," T-Bone said. "How the hell should I know?"

After that, things got worse. When T-Bone told her that he needed to "bench" their nightly frolic through the mysteries of love because he had to work on slugging and OBP (On Base Percentage) stats for some obscure players on some Triple A Team—The Pawtucket Hens—she had had enough and knew that *Sports Radio 650 WMOAN* was out to assassinate the few remaining brain cells T-Bone had left in his head (a bunch of those babies had gone south during *The Decade of Let's Have Another*) and she wasn't about to let the complete depletion of neural activity happen on her watch. T-Bone was more than a piece of meat.

In a quandary at first—embarrassed to talk to her friends and without the slightest sense of counselors or clergy—she turned to the *Yellow Pages*. At first, she didn't know what she was looking for. After making her way through a long list of divorce lawyers, she flipped back a few pages and landed on the guide word—Hypnotists. She scanned the list of registered hypnotherapists, discovering their willingness to stop and prevent in a single session smoking, drug use, weight gain, fear of flying, stress, and phobias. Unfortunately, no one advertised a fast acting "love trance" for an evaporating and volatile Romeo.

Still maybe (with *maybe* pumped with endurance of sand flies on their birthday) *a hypnotist might do T-Bone some good*, she thought, flipping through the pages again until coming to a section dedicated to schools—all kinds of schools, including academic, art, language, private, and religious. However, there seemed to be nothing-to-little there until her eyes caught a small 2" inch by 2" advertisement at the bottom right corner of the "language" page. Across a black field, she read the white letters, *Love School*, underscored by the simple command: *Turn him back to a real lover*.

The day Molly dropped T-Bone

off at the Love School, he had just finished calculating the average speed of the fastball by set up men (7th and 8th inning pitchers) in the American and National Leagues since the invention and implementation of the radar gun to register speed of delivery.

"Can you believe it, Molly," he said. "The average in the American League is a pitiful 84.5 mph, while over in the NL the rate of speed is 90.2 mph."

"That's lovely, T-Bone," Molly said, guiding him up the stairs of what was obviously a gaudy McMansion on the elite side of town.

Unaware of his surroundings, T-Bone continued:

"That's pretty much the difference between a change up and a fastball, yet we're just talking only fastballs here."

A chill ran up and down Molly's spine when she rang the bell and detected the melody of "Love Stinks" ("I've been through diamonds…I've been through rings…I've been through it all….LS…yeah, yeah… LS") echo through the house. Maybe it was time to split. Maybe T-Bone would prefer fixing his eyes on a pendulum of time. Maybe clucking like a chicken wouldn't be all that bad. He was a fan of the Pawtucket Hens, wasn't he?

Decisions, decisions, she thought, biting into an index finger in anticipation of the peppermint-striped door opening.

When Mr. and Mrs. Lovefest finally opened the grand and gauche door, they greeted their new customers with compassionate smiles. Veterans of love, they had seen the panic in the eyes of an "owner" on numerous occasions before dropping off their "friend" for some necessary love work and knew that compassion calmed the nerves of new clients. Assured that T-Bone really didn't know where the hell he was (OK, he was flashing a complicated set of signs – ear tugs, nose rubs, crotch grabs, knee taps – for stealing an imaginary base), they fixed their gaze on Molly, intensifying their compassionate grins to match the energy of her teeth in her finger.

And then, while Mr. Lovefest (appropriately attired in navy blue blazer with a pomegranate cravat, linen slacks, and loafers with tassels) thanked Molly for faxing important information about T-Bone to them, Mrs. Lovefest (appropriately attired in a sheer see-through blouse and cut-off jeans) snapped a smart and stylish rhinestone collar (with leash) around T-Bone's neck. Leading him through the door (one could now detect soft music and scents of jasmine incense) via a gentle tug on the imitation leather leash, she turned back to Molly, saying:

"Give me a couple of weeks, at least, with this love puppy. Then call us."

PICTOPOESY (cont.)

by Joel Lipman

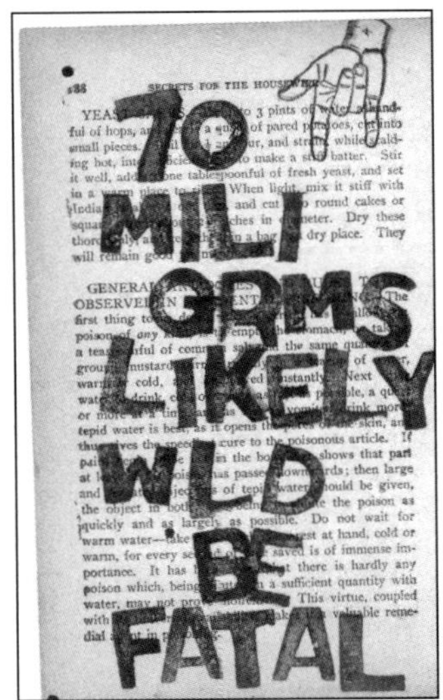

WOKE UP
WHO LIVES
WILL SEE
CONTENTS
Liquid
Fragile
Perishable
Hazardous
None Of The Above

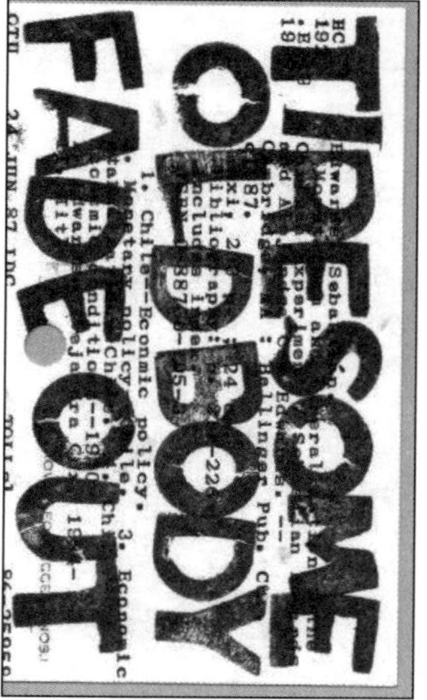
TIRESOME
OLD BODY
FADE OUT

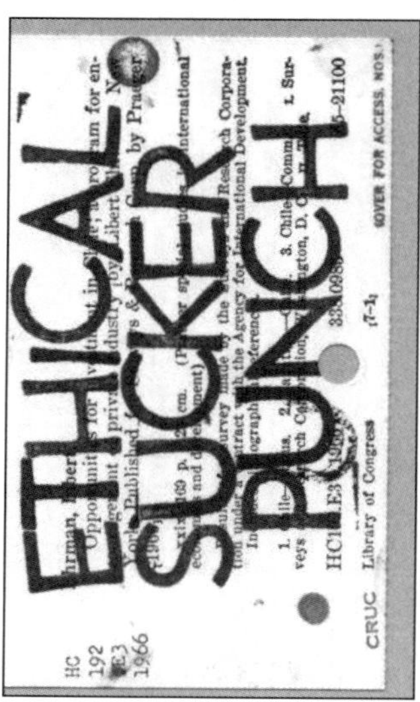
ETHICAL
SUCKER
PUNCH
CRUC Library of Congress

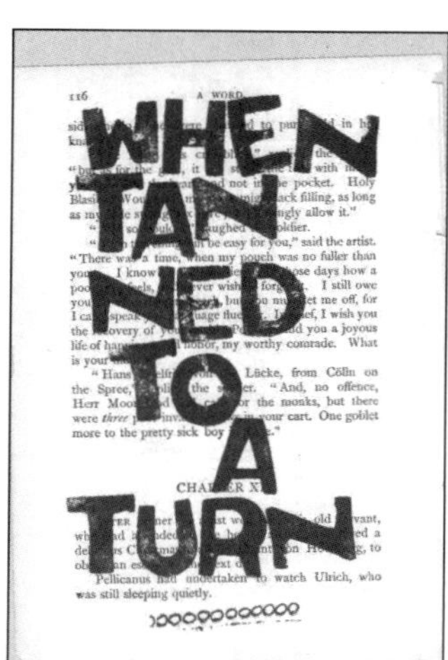
WHEN
TAN
NED
TO
A
TURN

LONE
PEEP
HOLE
DI
AG
NO
SIS
CLAIM CHECK
458
458
HAT
CHECK
POEM
HYGIENE
SCREAM

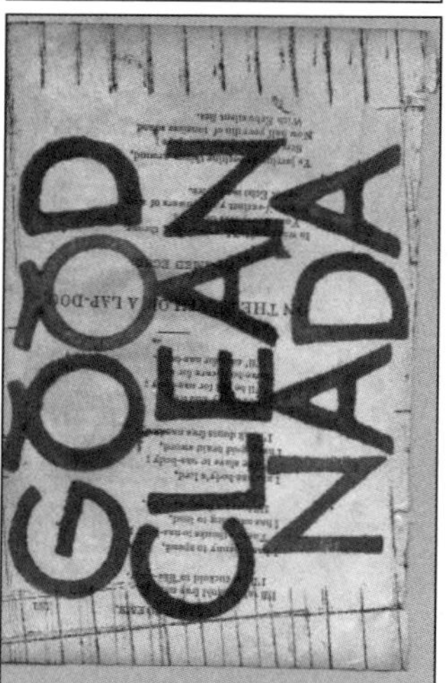
GOOD
CLEAN
NADA

DE PORT
MORPH
INE
FLES H
ITEM

THE WART OF SATAN

by Adrian C. Louis

> "Never bring the Lord an animal that
> is blind, has broken bones, cuts, warts, scabs,
> or ringworm. Never give the Lord any of these in
> a sacrifice by fire on the altar."
> —LEVITICUS 22:22

I offered my broken spirit
to the Lord and he ignored
me so I swam inexorably
towards the black light.

Somewhere between immaculate
conception & wireless reception,
the Wart of Satan was born. Oh,
fearsome wart, I am old & tired.
Talk down & dirty to me.

Blessed be your "snow day"
inception when I was alone
at home with the tube
& the lube & finished,
trumped the desperation
of the Last Supper with
homemade beef stew
aged in the freezer for
two wartless years.

The boxer interviewed said,
"I want to inflict damage
once I step into the ring."
The Wart of Satan comprehends
all snot-knocking epiphanies.

In Leviticus, it says, "When
a wart becomes bed bound
upon your nose, do not despair.
It has only chosen a cushy coffin."

In the soulless desert of
faux-quaint Minnesota, I hear
a homely Pillsbury doughboy
on Public Radio moaning
the blues so far off-key that
winos puking blood would
be sweeter music to me.
Wart of Satan, go thee to him.
Go thee to the Rolling Stones
who wiggle their wrinkled
wieners at the Super Bowl.

Not that it matters, but
in Leviticus it also speaks
of a green, green valley
where two bears danced
down a road covered
with dusty toads, each
step an explosion of toad
ghosts & warts.

Blessed be the dawn
& its expurgation
of historical facts.
But how should I react
to the minor cruelty of
a devil's ship, a Mayflower
landing upon my nose?

The store bought remedy
is not poetical & quite
unlike a needed scalping.
It's more like peeling back
the skullcap & peeing
on one's brain. This is
your brain on drugs.

Of course there are
no atheists in foxholes.
I am no snitch & I
am no bitch (simply
something of a witch
with a cursed proboscis)
but I am going to kill
the Wart of Satan.

Poof.
Gone.
Merely a whisper
in my silver sky of age.
My flesh fluttered, rose,
tasted rain & stalled in
morose lack of movement.
You came with the dust…
& were gone with the wind.

This bereavement
is awkwardly odd.
Caught in a graceless angle
of vanity, I was weak
when I wanted you gone.
Wart, you most surely
were flesh of my flesh
& a fla sh of my ashes.

CARVILLE, LOUISIANA:
VILLAGE OF FORGOTTEN NAMES

by Megan Burns

in Carville
    the largest continental leprosarium
    fondly called "Carville"

three types of leprosy
    the most prevalent
affected the skin first and the nerves later
            called itself lepromatous
            called itself hansen's disease
mycobacterium leprae
            called itself la maladie que tu nommes pas
but what's in a name

think of your family
back at home
and
their
terrible
shame

            (long incubation 3-5 years or as long as 20)

think of the monkeys in the monkey house
think of the emperor sulking in his pavillion
& he has everything
think of the plain yellow light
think of the coyotito singing the world into existence

    no little altars, there are candles burning
there is no supplication
    only the mystery of the flesh
        body, tongue

the small gods, happy with the sacrifice,
    dance in their caves
it's the other gods who dive for glory
  go unrecognized here

    where there is no transubstantiation
each day no one is saved from their common fate
  there are no miracles
        to stun the crowd
            no one calls the dead
                from their resting place
no one puts back on the fingers and toes
        or turns the stench into a sweet perfume
no one uncovers the eye and looks and looks
        straight down into the soul

no identification papers are needed to get in here

1894 the first patients arrive
Dec. 1 1894 in the middle of the night
by barge

"In the Middle Ages, the leper was a social text in which corruption was made visible, an emblem of decay."
- Sontag, *Illness as Metaphor*

genetic susceptibility confirmed
9 banded armadillos
5% have naturally occurring leprosy
a symbol
for leprosy research
the 9 banded armadillo

skin of leather, jump up like a rabbit when you step on it
out in the field behind mamie's house out here they like weeds
peppering the side of the road with them upturn'd corpses
there one, there one, there one, come and see 'em

the armadillo on the doubloon
turned head over tail
Mardi Gras day
in the parade they held at Carville
for those who never left

Carville closed in 1999
from Federally regulated hospital to state: the passing of land and building, of sanctum and home who owns the health and services of the patients of the occupants of the lives lived out in disarray but where is the location of this emotion that sounds betrayed

[the patients] they are still very much a large part and the heart of this facility
at the heart of the matter

in 2002 the building became home to a Southern anti-terrorism Training Academy

Will Carville have a second century of glory?
depends on the state
of your skin

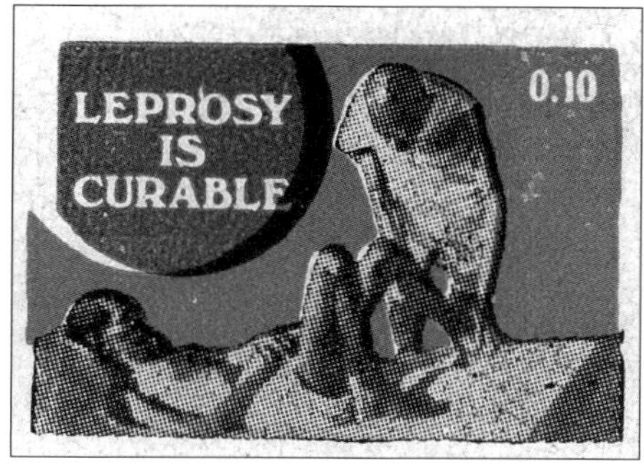

NEW ORLEANS: THE ART OF THE CORPSE

by Andrei Codrescu

When New Orleanians returned to their homes after the Storm they were struck by a smell that has no equivalent in recent American history: a stupefying blend of decaying animal flesh as layered as the city's history. The sweet rankness of animal and human death floated around the city like it might have in the aftermath of a Yellow Fever epidemic of the 18th century, but added to it was the putrid efflorescence of 20th century grocery store meat blossoming inside thousands of refrigerators. For a week or so after the Storm, when the city wallowed in its filth and misery without help from the United States of America, which they had mistakenly believed they were part of, people helped each other drag the taped-up fridges unto the street. Rows and rows of white metal boxes cradling generations of maggots began to fill the narrow streets of America's oldest city. Waves of putrefaction rolled over the streets. New Orleans sank into the funk like a corpse into the embrace of the earth. The rows of fridges lining the streets looked by moonlight like primed canvasses ready for painting. The city's artists, who have been enthralled since John James Audubon by New Orleans' embrace of decay and death (Audubon purchased American birds dead from the French Market) were not long in reacting. New Orleans music and art had always been inspired by funk: rotting vegetation, blooming night jasmine, the faint smell of the dead wafting from the city's above-ground cemeteries, rotting crustaceans, transpiration, and sex. Now here was all this funk, magnified a thousand times. And here were all these metal tombs stretching as far as the eye could see, more numerous than the graves they resembled.
The art appeared instantly and it was, appropriately, political. "Chem Trails Are Real: Weather Control is Here," was scrawled below a jet leaving behind what looked like a trail of poison. Another fridge warned severely: "Do Not Open: Cheney Inside." Inside others one could find Bush, Rice, Nagin, and Michael Brown doing obscene things within with the maggots and with each other. In a short time, there were thousands of art works in the city, an exhibition that stretched for miles, that had no official opening, that was constantly in progress. Today, most of the show is closed. National Guardsmen, volunteers, and city workers have incinerated the art after hauling it to vast refrigerator graveyards. New Orleans always renewed its armies of ghosts after every disaster of its 500-year history, but this last addition came with its own unique, absolutely new style.

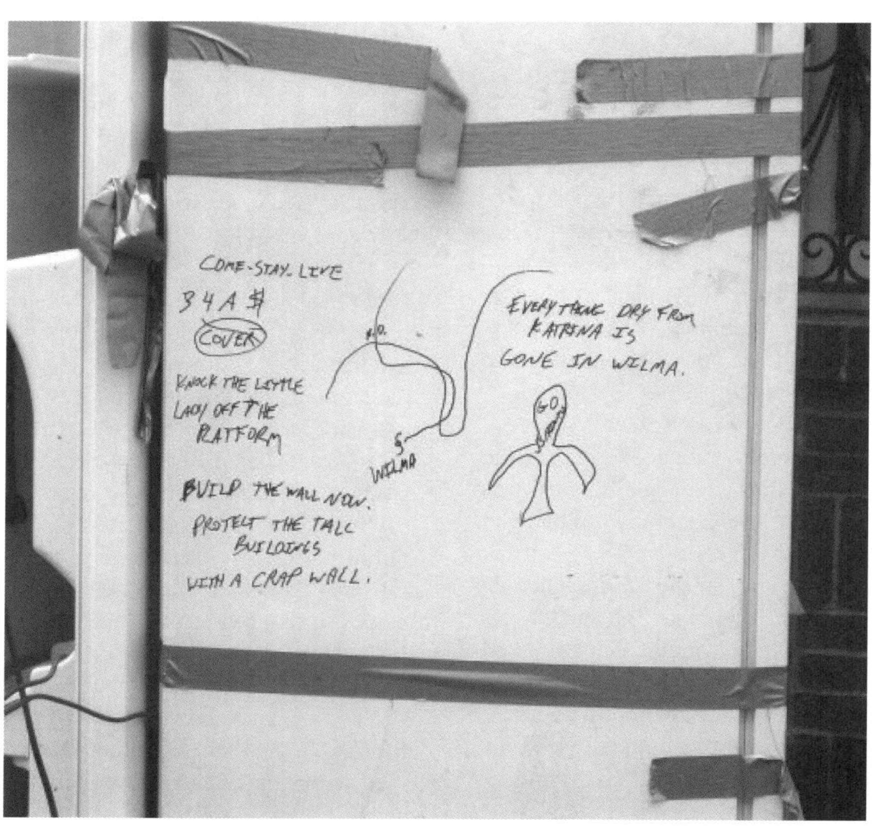
COME-STAY-LIVE
3 4 A $
COVER
KNOCK THE LITTLE
LADY OFF THE
PLATFORM
N.O.
WILMA
BUILD THE WALL NOW.
PROTECT THE TALL
BUILDINGS
WITH A CRAP WALL.
EVERYTHING DRY FROM
KATRINA IS
GONE IN WILMA.
GOD

SOLD
Fashion
God
INSIDE
Do Not
OPEN!

Rice & Nagin inside

Do Not Open

Cheney, Bush,
Blanco & Nagin & Rice
Gettin' Bussy
Do not open

BOOKS
NOW!
IRON RAIL
LIBRARY
511 MARIGNY

LOVE

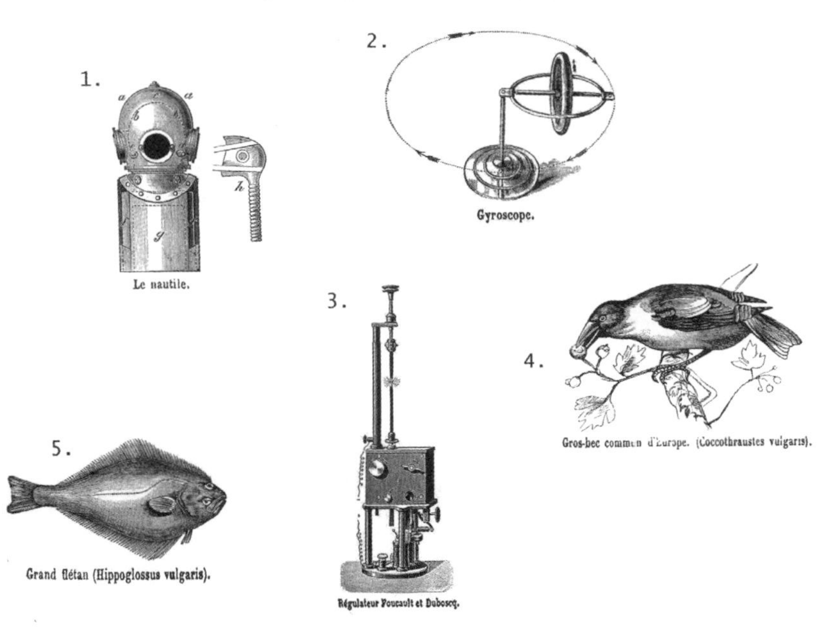
1.
Le nautile.
2.
Gyroscope.
3.
Régulateur Foucault et Duboscq.
4.
Gros-bec commun d'Europe. (Coccothraustes vulgaris).
5.
Grand flétan (Hippoglossus vulgaris).

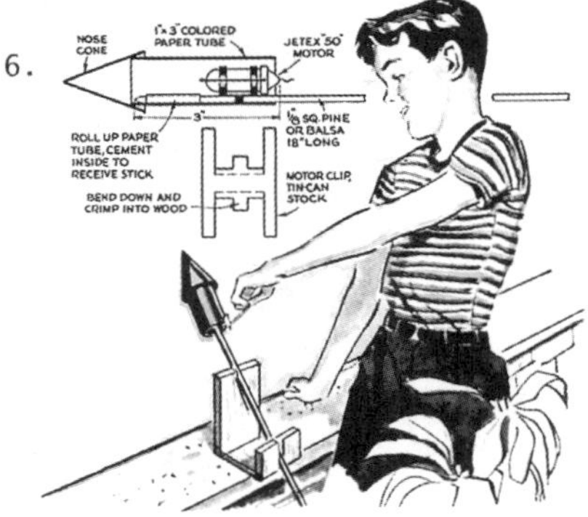
6.
NOSE CONE
1"x3" COLORED PAPER TUBE
JETEX "50" MOTOR
3"
1/8" SQ. PINE OR BALSA 18" LONG
ROLL UP PAPER TUBE, CEMENT INSIDE TO RECEIVE STICK
MOTOR CLIP, TIN-CAN STOCK
BEND DOWN AND CRIMP INTO WOOD

Exquisite Corpse Annual is published through the
University of Central Arkansas for Culture Shock Foundation, Inc.
We are grateful for funding from the UCA Foundation, the College of
Fine Arts and Communication, and the Department of Writing at UCA.
Please address all correspondence for the Annual to
corpse_ed@yahoo.com or send to:

Exquisite Corpse Annual
Department of Writing
University of Central Arkansas
Conway, AR 72035

Submissions for the Annual can be sent to the address above and should include a SASE. At this time, the Annual is not accepting submissions via email. Email submissions may be sent for consideration to our online sister journal (guidelines available at www.corpse.org).

Copies of the Annual are available through Amazon.com, Small Press Distribution (www.spdbooks.org) or they can be purchased at a discount by sending a check for $15.00 directly to the address above. Make checks payable to "UCA."

Tax-exempt contributions
to the Annual can be made by going to
www.uca.edu/campaign/onlinegiving.php
Just hit the online giving link & enter
"for Exquisite Corpse Annual"
in the comments section.

www.corpse.org